Participative Management

PARTICIPATIVE MANAGEMENT

A Harvard Business Review Paperback

The *Harvard Business Review* articles in this collection are available as individual reprints. Discounts apply to quantity purchases. For information and ordering contact Operations Department, Harvard Business School Publishing Division, Boston, MA 02163. Telephone: (617) 495-6192, 9 a.m. to 5 p.m. ET. Fax: (617) 495-6985, 24 hours a day.

© 1984, 1985, 1986, 1987, 1988, 1989, 1990, 1991 by the President and Fellows of Harvard College.

Editor's Note: Some articles in this book may have been written before authors and editors began to take into consideration the role of women in management. We hope the archaic usage representing all managers as male does not detract from the usefulness of the collection.

All rights reserved. No part of this book may be reproduced, stored in a retrieval system, or transmitted, in any form or by any means, electronic, mechanical, photocopying, recording, or otherwise, without the prior written permission of the copyright holder.
Printed in the United States of America.
93 92   5 4 3 2

Contents

The Collaborative Organization

Democracy Is Inevitable (An HBR Classic)
Philip Slater and Warren G. Bennis
3

First published in 1964, this article argues that democracy is inevitable, in both the workplace and the world. The reason: as a social system, it is adaptable to chronic change; as a form of business organization, it is best suited to accommodate technological change. (September–October 1990)

The Coming of the New Organization
Peter F. Drucker
13

The large business 20 years hence is more likely to resemble a hospital or a symphony than a typical hierarchical organization of today. The new organization will be composed of specialists who direct and discipline their own performance. (January–February 1988)

Matrix Management: Not a Structure, a Frame of Mind
Christopher A. Bartlett and Sumantra Ghoshal
23

An elaborate matrix organization can impair a company's ability to stay light on its feet. The matrix can be untangled and rewoven into a new fabric of strong central values and vigorous decentralized action. (July–August 1990)

The New Managerial Work
Rosabeth Moss Kanter
31

Managers must collaborate with the people they manage and build relationships across the organization as hierarchy fades and corporations become more flexible. (November–December 1989)

Entrepreneurship Reconsidered: The Team as Hero
Robert B. Reich
39

The problem with the dominant myth of the self-reliant entrepreneur is its obsolescence. In collective entrepreneurship, the capacity of work teams to innovate becomes something greater than the sum of its parts. (May–June 1987)

Wrestling with Jellyfish
Richard J. Boyle
47

An executive with a large firm that shifted from Patton-style management to a participatory model found it a slippery business. He shares the throes of the transition and ways of "putting structure in the jellyfish." (January–February 1984)

In Praise of Hierarchy
Elliott Jaques
57

After 3,000 years of success, managerial hierarchy has not had its day. The key to organizational success is individual accountability. Hierarchy preserves unambiguous accountability for getting work done. (January–February 1990)

Participation on the Factory Floor

From Control to Commitment in the Workplace
Richard E. Walton
67

Both companies and individuals benefit when management stimulates worker commitment by giving manufacturing employees broad responsibilities and a meaningful role in decision making. (March–April 1985)

People Policies for the New Machines
Richard E. Walton and Gerald I. Susman
75

Old-line management styles and advanced manufacturing technology are not a good fit. The new machines require alert, multiskilled operators, interactive work groups, floor-level decision making, and innovative management. (March–April 1987)

The Human Costs of Manufacturing Reform
Janice A. Klein
85

New manufacturing systems entail greater worker responsibility. But increased responsibility does not mean increased discretion over time and work. The author suggests ways of managing the surprise and disillusionment. (March–April 1989)

Good Supervisors Are Good Supervisors—Anywhere
Janice A. Klein and Pamela A. Posey
91

Effective supervisors in a traditional hierarchical organization can become excellent team leaders in the new participative work systems. (November–December 1986)

Managing without Managers
Ricardo Semler
96

A Brazilian manufacturing firm has no hierarchy and lets workers set their own hours and vote on important corporate decisions. The firm may be an anomaly, but it is a successful—and happy—one. (September–October 1989)

How I Learned to Let My Workers Lead
Ralph Stayer
106

The head of a successful but vulnerable family business decided to make some changes. Starting with himself, he slowly delegated his nearly complete control to his employees. To his delight and dismay, the company flourished and he came to feel almost superfluous. (November–December 1990)

The Collaborative Organization

HBR CLASSIC

Democracy Is Inevitable

by Philip Slater and Warren G. Bennis

...because it is the only system that can successfully cope with the changing demands of contemporary civilization, in business as well as in government.

Cynical observers have always been fond of pointing out that business leaders who extol the virtues of democracy on ceremonial occasions would be the last to think of applying them to their own organizations. To the extent that this is true, however, it reflects a state of mind that is by no means peculiar to businesspeople but characterizes all Americans, if not perhaps all citizens of democracies.

This attitude is that democracy is a nice way of life for nice people, despite its manifold inconveniences—a kind of expensive and inefficient luxury, like owning a large medieval castle. Feelings about it are for the most part affectionate, even respectful, yet a little impatient. There are probably few people in the United States who have not at some time nourished in their hearts the blasphemous thought that life would go much more smoothly if democracy could be relegated to some kind of Sunday morning devotion.

The bluff practicality of the "nice but inefficient" stereotype masks a hidden idealism, however, for it implies that institutions can survive in a competitive environment through the sheer good-heartedness of those who maintain them. We challenge this notion. Even if all those benign sentiments were eradicated today, we would awaken tomorrow to find democracy still entrenched, buttressed by a set of economic, social, and political forces as practical as they are uncontrollable.

Philip Slater is artistic director of the Santa Cruz County Actors' Theatre. The author of many books and articles, his most recent book is Creative Chaos: Stumbling Toward Democracy, *to be published by Beacon Press in 1991. Warren G. Bennis is Distinguished Professor of Business Administration at the University of Southern California. His most recent book is* On Becoming a Leader *(Addison-Wesley, 1989). This article appeared originally in HBR March-April 1964.*

DRAWINGS BY MARIE-SOLANGE LADENIUS

Democracy has been so widely embraced not because of some vague yearning for human rights but because *under certain conditions* it is a more "efficient" form of social organization. (Our concept of efficiency includes the ability to survive and prosper.) It is not accidental that those nations of the world that have endured longest under conditions of relative wealth and stability are democratic, while authoritarian regimes have, with few exceptions, either crumbled or eked out a precarious and backward existence.

Despite this evidence, even so acute a statesman as Adlai Stevenson argued in a *New York Times* article on November 4, 1962, that the goals of the Communists are different from ours. "They are interested in power," he said, "we in community. With such fundamentally different aims, how is it possible to compare communism and democracy in terms of efficiency?"

Democracy (whether capitalistic or socialistic is not at issue here) is the only system that can successfully cope with the changing demands of contemporary civilization. We are not necessarily endorsing democracy as such; one might reasonably argue that industrial civilization is pernicious and should be abolished. We suggest merely that given a desire to survive in this civilization, democracy is the most effective means to this end.

Democracy Takes Over

There are signs that our business community is becoming aware of democracy's efficiency. Several of the newest and most rapidly blooming companies in the United States boast unusually democratic organizations. Even more surprising, some of the largest established corporations have been moving steadily, if accidentally, toward democratization. Feeling that administrative vitality and creativity were lacking in their systems of organization, they enlisted the support of social scientists and outside programs. The net effect has been to democratize their organizations. Executives and even entire management staffs have been sent to participate in human relations and organizational laboratories to learn skills and attitudes that ten years ago would have been denounced as anarchic and revolutionary. At these meetings, status prerogatives and traditional concepts of authority are severely challenged.

Many social scientists have played an important role in this development. The contemporary theories of McGregor, Likert, Argyris, and Blake have paved the way to a new social architecture. Research and training centers at the National Training Laboratories, Tavistock Institute, Massachusetts Institute of Technology, Harvard Business School, Boston University, University of California at Los Angeles, Case Institute of Technology, and others have pioneered in applying social science knowledge to improving organizational effectiveness. The forecast seems to hold genuine promise of progress.

System of Values. What we have in mind when we use the term "democracy" is not "permissiveness" or "laissez-faire" but a system of values – a climate of beliefs governing behavior – that people are internally compelled to affirm by deeds as well as words. These values include:

1. Full and free *communication*, regardless of rank and power.

2. A reliance on *consensus* rather than on coercion or compromise to manage conflict.

3. The idea that *influence* is based on technical competence and knowledge rather than on the vagaries of personal whims or prerogatives of power.

4. An atmosphere that permits and even encourages emotional *expression* as well as task-oriented behavior.

5. A basically *human* bias, one that accepts the inevitability of conflict between the organization and

> Adaptability to change has become the most important determinant of survival in American life.

the individual but is willing to cope with and mediate this conflict on rational grounds.

Changes along these dimensions are being promoted widely in U.S. industry. Most important for our analysis is what we believe to be the reason for these changes: *democracy becomes a functional necessity whenever a social system is competing for survival under conditions of chronic change.*

Adaptability to Change

Technological innovation is the most familiar variety of such change to the inhabitants of the modern world. But if change has now become a permanent and accelerating factor in American life, then adaptability to change becomes the most important determinant of survival. The profit, the saving, the efficiency, and the morale of the moment become secondary to keeping the door open for rapid readjustment to changing conditions.

Organization and communication research at MIT reveals quite dramatically what type of organization is best suited for which kind of environment. Specifically:

☐ For simple tasks under static conditions, an autocratic, centralized structure, such as has characterized most industrial organizations in the past, is quicker, neater, and more efficient.

☐ But for adaptability to changing conditions, for "rapid acceptance of a new idea," for "flexibility in dealing with novel problems, generally high morale and loyalty...the more egalitarian or decentralized type seems to work better." One of the reasons for this is that the centralized decision maker is "apt to discard an idea on the grounds that he is too busy or the idea too impractical."[1]

Our argument for democracy rests on an additional factor, one that is fairly complicated but profoundly important. Modern industrial organization has been based roughly on the antiquated system of the military. Relics of this can still be found in clumsy terminology such as "line and staff," "standard operating procedure," "table of organization," and so on. Other remnants can be seen in the emotional and mental assumptions regarding work and motivation held today by some managers and industrial consultants. By and large, these conceptions are changing, and even the military is moving away from the oversimplified and questionable assumptions on which its organization was originally based. Even more striking, as we have mentioned, are developments taking place in industry, no less profound than a fundamental move from the autocratic and arbitrary vagaries of the past toward democratic decision making.

This change has been coming about because of the palpable inadequacy of the military-bureaucratic model, particularly its response to rapid change, and because the institution of science is now emerging as a more suitable model.

Why is science gaining acceptance as a model? Not because we teach and conduct research within research-oriented universities. Curiously enough, universities have been resistant to democratization, far more so than most other institutions.

Science is winning out because the challenges facing modern enterprises are *knowledge*-gathering, *truth*-requiring dilemmas. Managers are not scientists, nor do we expect them to be. But the processes of problem solving, conflict resolution, and recognition of dilemmas have great kinship with the academic pursuit of truth. The institution of science is the only institution based on and geared for change. It is built not only to adapt to change but also to overthrow and create change. So it is—and will be—with modern industrial enterprises.

And here we come to the point. For the spirit of inquiry, the foundation of science, to grow and flourish, there must be a democratic environment. Science encourages a political view that is egalitarian, pluralistic, liberal. It accentuates freedom of opinion and dissent. It is against all forms of totalitarianism, dogma, mechanization, and blind obedience. As a prominent social psychologist has pointed out, "Men have asked for freedom, justice, and respect precisely as science has spread among them."[2] In short, the only way organizations can ensure a scientific attitude is to provide the democratic social conditions where one can flourish.

In other words, democracy in industry is not an idealistic conception but a hard necessity in those areas where change is ever present and creative scientific enterprise must be nourished. For democracy is the only system of organization that is compatible with perpetual change.

Retarding Factors

It might be objected here that we have been living in an era of rapid technological change for a hundred years, without any noticeable change in the average industrial company. True, there are many restrictions on the power of executives over their subordinates today compared with those prevailing at the end of the nineteenth century. But this hardly constitutes industrial democracy—the decision-making function is still an exclusive and jealously guarded prerogative of the top echelons. If democracy is an inevitable consequence of perpetual change, why have we not seen more dramatic changes in the structure of industrial organizations? The answer is twofold.

Obsolete Individuals. First, technological change is rapidly accelerating. We are now beginning an era when people's knowledge and approach can become obsolete before they have even begun the careers for which they were trained. We are living in an era of runaway inflation of knowledge and skill, where the value of what one learns is always slipping away. Perhaps this explains the feelings of futility, alienation, and lack of individual worth that are said to characterize our time.

Under such conditions, the individual *is* of relatively little significance. No matter how imaginative, energetic, and brilliant individuals may be, time will soon catch up with them to the point where they can profitably be replaced by others equally imaginative, energetic, and brilliant but with a more up-to-date viewpoint and fewer obsolete preconceptions. As Martin Gardner says about the difficulty some physicists have in grasping Einstein's theory of relativity: "If you are young, you have a great advantage over these scientists. Your mind has not yet developed those deep furrows along which thoughts so often are forced to travel."[3] This situation is just beginning to be felt as an immediate reality in U.S. industry, and it is this kind of uncontrollably rapid change that generates democratization.

Powers of Resistance. The second reason is that the mere existence of a dysfunctional tendency, such as the relatively slow adaptability of authoritarian structures, does not automatically bring about its disappearance. This drawback must first either be recognized for what it is or become so severe as to destroy the structures in which it is embedded. Both conditions are only now beginning to make themselves felt, primarily through the peculiar nature of modern technological competition.

The crucial change has been that the threat of technological defeat no longer comes necessarily from rivals within the industry, who usually can be imitated quickly without too great a loss, but often comes from outside—from new industries using new materials in new ways. One can therefore make no intelligent prediction about the next likely developments in industry. The blow may come from anywhere. Correspondingly, a viable corporation cannot merely develop and advance in the usual ways. To survive and grow, it must be prepared to go anywhere—to develop new products or techniques even if they are irrelevant to the present activities of the organization.[4] Perhaps that is why the beginnings of democratization have appeared most often in industries that depend heavily on invention, such as electronics. It is undoubtedly why more and more sprawling behemoths are planning consequential changes in their organizational structures and climates to release democratic potential.

Farewell to "Great Men"

The passing of years has also given the coup de grace to another force that retarded democratization—the "great man" who with brilliance and farsightedness could preside with dictatorial powers at the head of a growing organization and keep it at the vanguard of U.S. business. In the past, this person was usually a man with a single idea, or a constellation of related ideas, which he developed brilliantly. This is no longer enough.

Today, just as he begins to reap the harvest of his imagination, he finds himself suddenly outmoded because someone else (even perhaps one of his stodgier competitors, aroused by desperation) has carried the innovation a step further or found an entirely new and superior approach to it. How easily can he abandon his idea, which contains all his hopes, his ambitions, his very heart? His aggressiveness now begins to turn in on his own organization; and the absolutism of his position begins to be a liability, a dead hand on the flexibility and growth of the company. But the great man cannot be removed. In the short run, the company would even be hurt by his loss since its prestige derives to such an extent from his reputation. And by the time he has left, the organization will have receded into a secondary position within the industry. It might decay further when his personal touch is lost.

The "cult of personality" still exists, of course, but it is rapidly fading. More and more large corporations (General Motors, for one) predicate their growth not on "heroes" but on solid management teams.

Organization Men. Taking the place of the "great man," we are told, is the "organization man." Liberals and conservatives alike have shed many tears over this transition. The liberals have in mind as "the individual" some sort of creative deviant—an intellectual, artist, or radical politician. The conservatives are thinking of the old captains of industry and perhaps some great generals.

Neither is at all unhappy to lose the "individuals" mourned by the other, dismissing them contemptuously as Communists and rabblerousers on the one hand, criminals and Fascists on the other. What is particularly confusing in terms of the present issue is a tendency to equate conformity with autocracy—to see the new industrial organization as one in which all individualism is lost except for a few villainous, individualistic manipulators at the top.

But this, of course, is absurd in the long run. The trend toward the "organization man" is also a trend toward a looser and more flexible organization in which the roles to some extent are interchangeable and no one is indispensable. To many people, this trend is a monstrous nightmare, but one should not confuse it with the nightmares of the past. It may mean anonymity and homogeneity, but it does not and cannot mean authoritarianism, despite the bizarre anomalies and hybrids that may arise in a period of transition.

The reason it cannot is that it arises out of a need for flexibility and adaptability. Democracy and the dubious trend toward the "organization man" alike (for this trend is a part of democratization, whether we like it or not) arise from the need to maximize the availability of appropriate knowledge, skill, and insight under conditions of great variability.

Rise of the Professional. While the "organization man" idea has titillated the public imagination, it has masked a far more fundamental change now taking place; the rise of the "professional." Professional specialists, holding advanced degrees in such abstruse sciences as cryogenics or computer logic as well as in the more mundane business disciplines, are entering all types of organizations at a higher rate than any other sector of the labor market.

Such people seemingly derive their rewards from inner standards of excellence, from their professional societies, from the intrinsic satisfaction of their tasks. In fact, they are committed to the task, not the job; to their standards, not their boss. They are uncommitted except to the challenging environments where they can "play with problems."

These new professionals are remarkably compatible with our conception of a democratic system. For like them, democracy seeks no new stability, no end point; it is purposeless, save that it purports to ensure perpetual transition, constant alteration, ceaseless

> **Democracy attempts to upset nothing, but only to facilitate the potential upset of anything.**

instability. It attempts to upset nothing, but only to facilitate the potential upset of anything. Democracy and professionals identify primarily with the adaptive process, not the "establishment."

Yet all democratic systems are not entirely so—there are always limits to the degree of fluidity that can be borne. Thus it is not a contradiction to the theory of democracy to find that a particular democratic society or organization may be more "conservative" than an autocratic one. Indeed, the most dramatic, violent, and drastic changes have always taken place under autocratic regimes, for such changes usually require prolonged self-denial, while democracy rarely lends itself to such voluntary asceticism. But these changes have been viewed as finite and temporary, aimed at a specific set of reforms and moving toward a new state of nonchange. It is only when the society reaches a level of technological development at which survival is dependent on the institutionalization of perpetual change that democracy becomes necessary.

Reinforcing Factors

The Soviet Union is rapidly approaching this level and is beginning to show the effects, as we shall see. The United States has already reached it. Yet democratic institutions existed in the United States when it was still an agrarian nation. Indeed, democracy has existed in many places and at many times, long before the advent of modern technology. How can we account for these facts?

Expanding Conditions. First, it must be remembered that modern technology is not the only factor that could give rise to conditions of necessary perpetual change. Any situation involving rapid and unplanned expansion sustained over a sufficient period of time will tend to produce great pressure for democratization. Secondly, when we speak of democracy, we are referring not exclusively or

Retrospective Commentary

Looking back on this article, I am much less surprised that our prediction came true than that we had the chutzpah to make it. In the past 26 years, I have seen so many reasonable-sounding predictions bite the dust (including several of my own) that I have sworn off the habit altogether.

It's comforting to see that there are still predictable trends in our tangled world. It is especially gratifying to realize that the observations Warren and I made about the unsung efficiencies of democratic organization are even more true now than they were then (or than they were when Mary Parker Follett first made them half a century before that).

Some ideas in the article seem rather dated – the 1960s, after all, had scarcely begun. Our nostalgic farewell to the "cult of personality" was particularly premature – the national tendency to fawn over papier-mâché heroes shows little sign of having peaked. Moreover, the liberalizing trend in the Soviet Union under Khrushchev was just about to be soundly squelched. U.S. media are notoriously blind to long-term trends; to them, the Khrushchev era was over. In fact, it was by no means over.

It spawned a generation of leaders – Gorbachev and his cohorts – who realized the direction the Soviet Union would have to take and waited patiently for the opportunity to take it there.

The biggest surprise in the past quarter-century has been the deterioration of democracy in the United States and the resulting loss of its preeminent position among the nations of the world. Only in the most limited military sense can we still boast of being "number one." In all other respects – economic, social, scientific, technological, artistic – we are falling behind Europe and the Far East.

This loss of democratic vitality is a result of both the rigid, cold war mentality that has dominated government policymaking and the private sector's obsession with short-term profit. The executive branch of the U.S. government has become bloated, bureaucratized, overcentralized, and militarized to the point where comparisons with the Soviet Union are no longer tenuous. Democratic control over this behemoth has virtually disappeared. The checks and balances designed to prevent authoritarian rule have been subverted by executive power, and Congress has in effect surrendered to the president its power to declare war. All key national policies are now made secretly by an unelected body – the National Security Council – which operates in a manner indistinguishable from the Politburo.

Meanwhile, only a fraction of the population votes, and the outcome of most elections can be predicted by the amount of money spent by the candidates. The media have ceased to play an independent role – doing little more than uncritically relaying government handouts to the public.

And while our most progressive private enterprises are more democratically organized than when we wrote this article, the overriding trend in our society has been agglomeration, to the point where 1% of all corporations account for 87% of sales – a situation in which the word "private" no longer has substantive meaning.

A giant bureaucracy is cumbersome, inefficient, and allergic to change, no matter who runs it. This was our point 26 years ago, and society is paying a heavy price for having forgotten it.

– Philip Slater

---

even primarily to a particular political format. Indeed, American egalitarianism has perhaps its most important manifestation not in the Constitution but in the family.

Historians are fond of pointing out that Americans have always lived under expanding conditions – first the frontier, then the successive waves of immigration, now a runaway technology. The social effects of these kinds of expansion are of course profoundly different in many ways, but they share one impact: all have made it impossible for an authoritarian family system to develop on a large scale. Every foreign observer of American mores since the seventeenth century has commented that American children "have no respect for their parents," and every generation of Americans since 1650 has produced forgetful native moralists complaining about the decline in filial obedience and deference.

Descriptions of family life in colonial times make it quite clear that American parents were as easygoing, permissive, and child oriented then as now, and the children as independent and disrespectful. This lack of respect is not for the parents as individuals but for the concept of parental authority as such.

The basis for this loss of respect has been outlined quite dramatically by historian Oscar Handlin, who points out that in each generation of early settlers, the children were more at home in their new environment than their parents were – had less fear of the wilderness, fewer inhibiting European preconceptions and habits.[5] Furthermore, their parents were heavily dependent on them physically and economically. This was less true of the older families after the East became settled. But nearer the frontier, the conditions for familial democracy became again strikingly marked so that the cultural norm was protected from serious decay.

Further reinforcement came from new immigrants, who found their children better adapted to the world because of their better command of the language, better knowledge of the culture, better occupational opportunities, and so forth. It was the children who were expected to improve the social position of the family and who through their exposure to peer groups and the school system could act as intermediaries between their parents and the new world. It was not so much "American ways" that shook up the old family patterns as the demands and requirements of a new situation. How could the young look to the old as the ultimate fount of wisdom and knowledge when, in fact, their knowledge was irrelevant—when the children indeed had a better practical grasp of the realities of American life than did their elders?

The New Generation. These sources of reinforcement have now disappeared. But a third source has only just begun. Rapid technological change again means that the wisdom of elders is largely obsolete and that the young are better adapted to their culture than are their parents.

This fact reveals the basis for the association between democracy and change. The old, the learned, the powerful, the wealthy, those in authority—these are the ones who are committed. They have learned a pattern and succeeded in it. But when change comes, it is often the *uncommitted* who can best realize it and take advantage of it. This is why primogeniture has always lent itself so easily to social change in general and to industrialization in particular. The uncommitted younger children, barred from success in the older system, are always ready to exploit new opportunities. In Japan, younger sons were treated more indulgently by their parents and given more freedom to choose an occupation since "in Japanese folk wisdom, it is the younger sons who are the innovators."[6]

> **We underrate the strength of democracy because it creates an attitude of doubt, skepticism, and modesty.**

Democracy is a superior technique for making the uncommitted more available. The price it extracts is uninvolvement, alienation, and skepticism. The benefits that it gives are flexibility and the joy of confronting new dilemmas.

Doubt and Fears

Indeed, we may even in this way account for the poor opinion democracy has of itself. We underrate the strength of democracy because it creates a general attitude of doubt, skepticism, and modesty. It is only among the authoritarian that we find the dogmatic confidence, the self-righteousness, the intolerance and cruelty that permit one never to doubt oneself and one's beliefs. The looseness, sloppiness, and untidiness of democratic structures express the feeling that what has been arrived at today is probably only a partial solution and may well have to be changed tomorrow.

In other words, one cannot believe that change is in itself a good thing and still believe implicitly in the rightness of the present. Judging from the report of history, democracy has always underrated itself—one cannot find a democracy anywhere without also discovering (side by side with expressions of outrageous chauvinism) an endless pile of contemptuous and exasperated denunciations of it. (One of the key issues in our national politics today, as in the presidential campaign in 1960, is our "national prestige.") And perhaps this is only appropriate. For when a democracy ceases finding fault with itself, it has probably ceased to be a democracy.

Overestimating Autocracy. But feeling doubt about our own social system need not lead us to overestimate the virtues and efficiency of others. We can find this kind of overestimation in the exaggerated fear of the "Red Menace"—mere exposure to which is seen as leading to automatic conversion. Few authoritarians can conceive of the possibility that an individual could encounter an authoritarian ideology and not be swept away by it.

More widespread is the "better dead than Red" mode of thinking. Here again we find an underlying assumption that communism is socially, economically, and ideologically inevitable—that once the military struggle is lost, all is lost. Not only are these assumptions patently ridiculous; they also reveal a profound misconception about the nature of social systems. The structure of a society is not determined merely by a belief. It cannot be maintained if it does not work—that is, if no one, not even those in power, is benefiting from it. How many times in history have less civilized nations conquered more civilized ones only to be entirely transformed by the cultural influence of their victims? Do we then feel less civi-

Retrospective Commentary

It's wonderful—perhaps because it's so rare—to re-read something you wrote 26 years ago and discover you were right.

In 1990, after the extraordinary recent events in Eastern Europe, including the dismantling of the Berlin Wall, it seems obvious that democracy was inevitable. But 26 years ago, in the heat of the Cold War, it was not so certain. When Philip Slater and I first argued that democracy would eventually dominate in both the world and the workplace, a nuclear war between the United States and the Soviet Union seemed more likely than a McDonald's in Moscow.

Slater and I saw a common thread running through the most exciting organizations of the time: as the once-absolute power of top management atrophied, a more collegial organization where good ideas were valued even if they weren't the boss's was emerging. We were convinced democracy would triumph for a simple but utterly compelling reason—it worked. It was, and is, more effective than autocracy, bureaucracy, and other nondemocratic forms of organization.

It is only fair to note that in international politics, democratization is a very recent phenomenon, although a profound one. Only a year ago, Nicolae Ceausescu had the power to ban birth control in Romania and require that every typewriter be registered. The state even regulated the temperature of Romanian households. The events of recent months are even more remarkable because they were so long in coming. It was easier to speculate 26 years ago that democracy was inevitable than to imagine five months ago that the notoriously repressive military government of Myanmar, formerly Burma, would be ousted peacefully by the National League for Democracy, as it was in May of this year.

The democratization of the workplace has made fewer headlines but has been no less dramatic. In the 1960s, participative management was a radical enough notion that some of the Sloan fellows at MIT accused me of being a Communist for espousing it. Now most major corporations practice some form of egalitarian management. The pyramid-shaped organization chart has gone the way of the Edsel.

The change is pervasive. Self-managed work groups are replacing assembly lines in auto plants. Organizations as disparate as Herman Miller, the manufacturer of office furniture, and Beth Israel Hospital in Boston have adopted the democratic management techniques of the late Joseph Scanlon, one of the first to appreciate that employee involvement is crucial for quality control. At Hewlett-Packard's facility in Greeley, Colorado, most decisions are made not by traditional managers but by frontline employees who work in teams on parts of projects. Even project coordination is done by team representatives, working on committees known as "boards of directors."

No longer a monolith, the successful modern corporation is a Lego set whose parts can be readily reconfigured as circumstances change. The old paradigm that

---

lized than the Soviet Union? Is our system so brittle and theirs so enduring?

Actually, quite the contrary seems to be the case. For while democracy seems to be on a fairly sturdy basis in the United States (despite the efforts of self-appointed vigilantes to subvert it), there is considerable evidence that autocracy is beginning to decay in the Soviet Union.

Soviet Drift

Most Americans have great difficulty in evaluating the facts when they are confronted with evidence of decentralization in the Soviet Union, of relaxation of repressive controls, or of greater tolerance for criticism. We do not seem to sense the contradiction when we say that these changes were made in response to public discontent. For have we not also believed that an authoritarian regime, if efficiently run, can get away with ignoring the public's clamor?

There is a secret belief among us that either Khrushchev must have been mad to relax his grip or that it is all part of a secret plot to throw the West off guard: a plot too clever for naive Americans to fathom. It is seldom suggested that "de-Stalinization" took place because the rigid, repressive authoritarianism of the Stalin era was inefficient and that many additional relaxations will be forced upon the Soviet Union by the necessity of remaining amenable to technological innovation.

exalted control, order, and predictability has given way to a nonhierarchical order in which all employees' contributions are solicited and acknowledged and in which creativity is valued over blind loyalty. Sheer self-interest motivated the change. Organizations that encourage broad participation, even dissent, make better decisions. In a recent study, Rebecca A. Henry, a psychology professor at Purdue University, found that groups are better forecasters than are individuals. And the more the group disagrees initially, the more accurate the forecast is likely to be.

Slater and I were right on target, I think, in writing both that adaptability would become the most important determinant of an organization's survival and that information would drive the organization of the future. The person who has information wields more power than ever before. And even though industrial applications of the computer were still in their first decade, we sensed how important processing technology would be, largely, I suspect, because we were working in the Boston area, the birthplace of so much of the new technology.

I don't think we fully appreciated, however, the extent to which the new technology would accelerate the pace of change and help create a global corporation, if not a global village. With computers and fax machines, New York Life Insurance processes its claims not in New York or even the United States but in Ireland. Several years ago, I invited the Dalai Lama to participate in a seminar for CEOs at the University of Southern California. The embodiment of thousands of years of Tibetan spiritualism graciously declined by fax.

Slater and I failed to foresee one development that would profoundly change organizational life: the extraordinary role Japan would play in shaping U.S. corporate behavior in the 1980s. The discovery that another nation could challenge U.S. dominance in the marketplace inspired massive self-evaluation and forever disrupted the status quo. Nothing contributed more to the democratization of business than the belief, true or false, that Japanese management was more consensual than U.S. management. To meet Japanese competition, U.S. leaders were willing to do anything, even share their traditional prerogatives with subordinates.

So a new kind of leader has emerged who is a facilitator, not an autocrat, an appreciator of ideas, not necessarily a fount of them. The Great Man – or Woman – still exists as the public face of companies and countries, but the leader and the organization are no longer one and the same.

Around the world, the generals are being ousted and the poets are taking charge. Slater and I argued that the military-bureaucratic model was increasingly obsolete and was being replaced by a scientific model. That is still true. Science not only tolerates change; it creates change. And, as we wrote, science flourishes only in a democracy, the one form of organization recognizing that creativity, an invaluable commodity, is utterly unpredictable and can come from any quarter.

—Warren G. Bennis

But the inevitable Soviet drift toward a more democratic structure is not dependent on the realism of leaders. Leaders come from communities and families, and their patterns of thought are shaped by their experiences with authority in early life, as well as by their sense of what the traffic will bear. We saw that the roots of democracy in the United States were to be found in the nature of the American family. What does the Soviet family tell us in this respect?

Pessimism regarding the ultimate destiny of Soviet political life has always been based on the seemingly fathomless capacity of the Soviet people for authoritarian submission. Their tolerance for autocratic rulers was only matched by their autocratic family system, which, in its demand for filial obedience, was equal to those of Germany, China, and many Latin countries. Acceptance of authoritarian rule was based on this early experience in the family.

But modern revolutionary movements, both fascist and communist, have tended to regard the family with some suspicion, as the preserver of old ways and as a possible refuge from the State. Fascist dictators have extolled the conservatism of the family but tended at times to set up competitive loyalties for the young. Communist revolutionaries, on the other hand, have more unambivalently attacked family loyalty as reactionary and have deliberately undermined familial allegiances, partly to increase loyalty to the state, partly to facilitate industrialization and modernization by discrediting traditional mores.

Such destruction of authoritarian family patterns is a two-edged sword that eventually cuts away political as well as familial autocracy. The state may attempt to train submission in its own youth organizations, but so long as the family remains an institution, this earlier and more enduring experience will outweigh all others. And if the family has been forced by the state to be less authoritarian, the result is obvious.

In creating a youth that has a knowledge, a familiarity, and a set of attitudes more appropriate for successful living in the changing culture than those of its parents, the autocratic state has created a Frankensteinian monster that will eventually sweep away the authoritarianism in which it is founded. The Soviet Union's attempts during the late 1930s to reverse its stand on the family perhaps reflect some realization of this fact. Khrushchev's denunciations of certain Soviet artists and intellectuals also reflect fear of a process going further than what was originally intended.

A similar ambivalence has appeared in China, where the unforeseen consequences of the slogan "all for the children" recently produced a rash of articles stressing filial obligations. As W. J. Goode points out, "The propaganda campaign against the power of the elders may lead to misunderstanding on the part of the young, who may at times abandon their filial responsibilities to the State."[7]

Further, what the derogation of parental wisdom and authority has begun, the fierce drive for technological modernization will finish. Each generation of youth will be better adapted to the changing society than its parents were. And each generation of parents will feel increasingly modest and doubtful about overvaluing its wisdom and superiority as it recognizes the brevity of its usefulness.

We cannot, of course, predict what forms democratization might take in any nation of the world, nor should we become unduly optimistic about its impact on international relations. Although our thesis predicts the democratization of the entire globe, this is a view so long range as to be academic. There are infinite opportunities for global extermination before we reach any such stage of development.

We should expect that in the earlier stages of industrialization, dictatorial regimes will prevail in all of the less developed nations. And as we well know, autocracy is still highly compatible with a lethal if short-run military efficiency. We may expect many political grotesques, some of them dangerous in the extreme, to emerge during this long period of transition, as one society after another attempts to crowd the most momentous social changes into a generation or two, working from the most varied structural baselines.

But barring some sudden decline in the rate of technological change and on the (outrageous) assumption that war will somehow be eliminated during the next half-century, it is possible to predict that after this time, democracy will be universal. Each revolutionary autocracy, as it reshuffles the family structure and pushes toward industrialization, will sow the seeds of its own destruction, and democratization will gradually engulf it.

We might, of course, rue the day. A world of mass democracies may well prove homogenized and ugly. It is perhaps beyond human social capacity to maximize both equality and understanding on the one hand, diversity on the other. Faced with this dilemma, however, many people are willing to sacrifice quaintness to social justice, and we might conclude by remarking that just as Marx, in proclaiming the inevitability of communism, did not hesitate to give some assistance to the wheels of fate, so our thesis that democracy represents the social system of the electronic era should not bar these persons from giving a little push here and there to the inevitable.

References

1. W. G. Bennis, "Towards a 'Truly' Scientific Management: The Concept of Organization Health," *General Systems Yearbook*, December 1962, p. 273.

2. N. Sanford, "Social Science and Social Reform," Presidential Address for the Society for the Psychological Study of Social Issues at Annual Meeting of the American Psychological Association, Washington, D.C., August 28, 1958.

3. *Relativity for the Million* (New York: The Macmillan Company, 1962), p. 11.

4. For a fuller discussion of this trend, see Theodore Levitt, "Marketing Myopia," HBR July-August 1960, p. 45.

5. *The Uprooted* (Boston: Little, Brown and Company, 1951).

6. W. J. Goode, *World Revolution and Family Patterns* (New York: Free Press, 1963), p. 355.

7. Ibid., pp. 313-15.

Reprint 90510

THE COMING OF THE NEW ORGANIZATION

by PETER F. DRUCKER

The typical large business 20 years hence will have fewer than half the levels of management of its counterpart today, and no more than a third the managers. In its structure, and in its management problems and concerns, it will bear little resemblance to the typical manufacturing company, circa 1950, which our textbooks still consider the norm. Instead it is far more likely to resemble organizations that neither the practicing manager nor the management scholar pays much attention to today: the hospital, the university, the symphony orchestra. For like them, the typical business will be knowledge-based, an organization composed largely of specialists who direct and discipline their own performance through organized feedback from colleagues, customers, and headquarters. For this reason, it will be what I call an information-based organization.

Businesses, especially large ones, have little choice but to become information-based. Demographics, for one, demands the shift. The center of gravity in employment is moving fast from manual and clerical workers to knowledge workers who resist the command-and-control model that business took from the military 100 years ago. Economics also dictates change, especially the need for large businesses to innovate and to be entrepreneurs. But above all, information technology demands the shift.

Advanced data-processing technology isn't necessary to create an information-based organization, of course. As we shall see, the British built just such an organization in India when "information technology" meant the quill pen, and barefoot runners were the "telecommunications" systems. But as advanced technology becomes more and more prevalent, we have to engage in analysis and

Peter F. Drucker is Marie Rankin Clarke Professor of Social Sciences and Management at the Claremont Graduate School, which recently named its management center after him. Widely known for his work on management practice and thought, he is the author of numerous articles and books, the most recent of which is The Frontiers of Management *(E.P. Dutton/Truman Talley Books, 1986). This is Mr. Drucker's twenty-fourth contribution to HBR.*

The large business 20 years hence is more likely to resemble a hospital or a symphony than a typical manufacturing company.

diagnosis—that is, in "information"—even more intensively or risk being swamped by the data we generate.

So far most computer users still use the new technology only to do faster what they have always done before, crunch conventional numbers. But as soon as a company takes the first tentative steps from data to information, its decision processes, management structure, and even the way its work gets done begin to be transformed. In fact, this is already happening, quite fast, in a number of companies throughout the world.

We can readily see the first step in this transformation process when we consider the impact of computer technology on capital-investment decisions. We have known for a long time that there is no one right way to analyze a proposed capital investment. To understand it we need at least six analyses: the expected rate of return; the payout period and the investment's expected productive life; the discounted present value of all returns through the productive lifetime of the investment; the risk in not making the investment or deferring it; the cost and risk in case of failure; and finally, the opportunity cost. Every accounting student is taught these concepts. But before the advent of data-processing capacity, the actual analyses would have taken man-years of clerical toil to complete. Now anyone with a spreadsheet should be able to do them in a few hours.

The availability of this information transforms the capital-investment analysis from opinion into diagnosis, that is, into the rational weighing of alternative assumptions. Then the information transforms the capital-investment decision from an opportunistic, financial decision governed by the numbers into a business decision based on the probability of alternative strategic assumptions. So the decision both presupposes a business strategy and challenges that strategy and its assumptions. What was once a budget exercise becomes an analysis of policy.

Information transforms a budget exercise into an analysis of policy.

The second area that is affected when a company focuses its data-processing capacity on producing information is its organization structure. Almost immediately, it becomes clear that both the number of management levels and the number of managers can be sharply cut. The reason is straightforward: it turns out that whole layers of management neither make decisions nor lead. Instead, their main, if not their only, function is to serve as "relays"—human boosters for the faint, unfocused signals that pass for communication in the traditional pre-information organization.

One of America's largest defense contractors made this discovery when it asked what information its top corporate and operating managers needed to do their jobs. Where did it come from? What form was it in? How did it flow? The search for answers soon revealed that whole layers of management—perhaps as many as 6 out of a total of 14—existed only because these questions had not been asked before. The company had had data galore. But it had always used its copious data for control rather than for information.

Information is data endowed with relevance and purpose. Converting data into information thus requires knowledge. And knowledge, by definition. is specialized. (In fact, truly knowledgeable people tend toward overspecialization, whatever their field, precisely because there is always so much more to know.)

The information-based organization requires far more specialists overall than the command-and-control companies we are accustomed to. Moreover, the specialists are found in operations, not at corporate headquarters. Indeed, the operating organization tends to become an organization of specialists of all kinds.

Information-based organizations need central operating work such as legal counsel, public relations, and labor relations as much as ever. But the need for service staffs—that is, for people without operating responsibilities who only advise, counsel, or coordinate—shrinks drastically. In its *central* management, the information-based organization needs few, if any, specialists.

Because of its flatter structure, the large, information-based organization will more closely resemble the businesses of a century ago than today's big companies. Back then, however, all the knowledge, such as it was, lay with the very top people. The rest were helpers or hands, who mostly did the same work and did as they were told. In the information-based organization, the knowledge will be primarily at the bottom, in the minds of the specialists who do different work and direct themselves. So today's typical organization in which knowledge tends to be concentrated in service staffs, perched rather insecurely between top management and the operating people, will likely be labeled a phase, an attempt to infuse knowledge from the top rather than obtain information from below.

Finally, a good deal of work will be done differently in the information-based organization. Traditional departments will serve as guardians of standards, as centers for training and the assignment of specialists; they won't be where the work gets done. That will happen largely in task-focused teams.

This change is already under way in what used to be the most clearly defined of all departments—research. In pharmaceuticals, in telecommunications, in papermaking, the traditional *sequence* of research, development, manufacturing, and marketing is being replaced by *synchrony*: specialists from all these functions work together as a team, from the inception of research to a product's establishment in the market.

How task forces will develop to tackle other business opportunities and problems remains to be seen. I suspect, however, that the need for a task force, its assignment, its composition, and its leadership will have to be decided on case by case. So the organization that will be developed will go beyond the matrix and may indeed be quite different from it. One thing is clear, though: it will require greater self-discipline and even greater emphasis on individual responsibility for relationships and for communications.

Traditional departments won't be where the work gets done.

To say that information technology is transforming business enterprises is simple. What this transformation will require of companies and top managements is much harder to decipher. That is why I find it helpful to look for clues in other kinds of information-based organizations, such as the hospital, the symphony orchestra, and the British administration in India.

A fair-sized hospital of about 400 beds will have a staff of several hundred physicians and 1,200 to 1,500 paramedics divided among some 60 medical and paramedical specialities. Each specialty has its own knowledge, its own training, its own language. In each specialty, especially the paramedical ones like the clinical lab and physical therapy, there is a head person who is a working specialist rather than a full-time manager. The head of each specialty reports directly to the top, and there is little middle management. A good deal of the work is done in ad hoc teams as required by an individual patient's diagnosis and condition.

A large symphony orchestra is even more instructive, since for some works there may be a few hundred musicians on stage playing together. According to organization theory then, there should be several group vice president conductors and perhaps a half-dozen division VP conductors. But that's not how it works. There is only the conductor-CEO—and every one of the musicians plays directly to that person without an intermediary. And each is a high-grade specialist, indeed an artist.

But the best example of a large and successful information-based organization, and one without any middle management at all, is the British civil administration in India.[1]

The British ran the Indian subcontinent for 200 years, from the middle of the eighteenth century through World War II, without making any fundamental changes in organization structure or administrative policy. The Indian civil service never had more than 1,000 members to administer the vast and densely populated subcontinent—a tiny fraction (at most 1%) of the legions of Confucian mandarins and palace eunuchs employed next door to administer a not-much-more populous China. Most of the Britishers were quite young; a 30-year-old was a survivor, especially in the early years. Most lived alone in isolated outposts with the nearest countryman a day or two of travel away, and for the first hundred years there was no telegraph or railroad.

The organization structure was totally flat. Each district officer reported directly to the "Coo," the provincial political secretary. And since there were nine provinces, each political secretary had at least 100 people reporting directly to him, many times what the doctrine of the span of control would allow. Nevertheless, the system worked remarkably well, in large part because it was designed to ensure that each of its members had the information he needed to do his job.

Each month the district officer spent a whole day writing a full report to the political secretary in the provincial capital. He discussed each of his principal tasks—there were only four, each clearly delineated. He put down in detail what he had expected would happen with respect to each of them, what actually did happen, and why, if there was a discrepancy, the two differed. Then he wrote down what he expected would happen in the ensuing month with respect to each key task and what he was going to do about it, asked questions about policy, and commented on long-term opportunities, threats, and needs. In turn, the political secretary "minuted" every one of those reports—that is, he wrote back a full comment.

The best example of a large and successful information-based organization had no middle management at all.

---

1. The standard account is Philip Woodruff, *The Men Who Ruled India*, especially the first volume, *The Founders of Modern India* (New York: St. Martin's, 1954). How the system worked day by day is charmingly told in *Sowing* (New York: Harcourt Brace Jovanovich, 1962), volume one of the autobiography of Leonard Woolf (Virginia Woolf's husband).

On the basis of these examples, what can we say about the requirements of the information-based organization? And what are its management problems likely to be? Let's look first at the requirements. Several hundred musicians and their CEO, the conductor, can play together because they all have the same score. It tells both flutist and timpanist what to play and when. And it tells the conductor what to expect from each and when. Similarly, all the specialists in the hospital share a common mission: the care and cure of the sick. The diagnosis is their "score"; it dictates specific action for the X-ray lab, the dietitian, the physical therapist, and the rest of the medical team.

Information-based organizations, in other words, require clear, simple, common objectives that translate into particular actions. At the same time, however, as these examples indicate, information-based organizations also need concentration on one objective or, at most, on a few.

Because the "players" in an information-based organization are specialists, they cannot be told how to do their work. There are probably few orchestra conductors who could coax even one note out of a French horn, let alone show the horn player how to do it. But the conductor can focus the horn player's skill and knowledge on the musicians' joint performance. And this focus is what the leaders of an information-based business must be able to achieve.

Yet a business has no "score" to play by except the score it writes as it plays. And whereas neither a first-rate performance of a symphony nor a miserable one will change what the composer wrote, the performance of a business continually creates new and different scores against which its performance is assessed. So an information-based business must be structured around goals that clearly state management's performance expectations for the enterprise and for each part and specialist and around organized feedback that compares results with these performance expectations so that every member can exercise self-control.

The other requirement of an information-based organization is that everyone take information responsibility. The bassoonist in the orchestra does so every time she plays a note. Doctors and paramedics work with an elaborate system of reports and an information center, the nurse's station on the patient's floor. The district officer in India acted on this responsibility every time he filed a report.

The key to such a system is that everyone asks: Who in this organization depends on me for what information? And on whom, in turn, do I depend? Each person's list will always include superiors and subordinates. But the most important names on it will be those of colleagues, people with whom one's primary relationship is coordination. The relationship of the internist, the surgeon, and the anesthesiologist is one example. But the relationship of a biochemist, a pharmacologist, the medical director in charge of clinical testing, and a marketing specialist in a pharmaceutical company is no different. It, too, requires each party to take the fullest information responsibility.

Information responsibility to others is increasingly understood, especially in middle-sized companies. But information responsibility to oneself is still largely neglected. That is, everyone in an organization should constantly be thinking through what information he or she needs to do the job and to make a contribution.

Who depends on me for information? And on whom do I depend?

This may well be the most radical break with the way even the most highly computerized businesses are still being run today. There, people either assume the more data, the more information—which was a perfectly valid assumption yesterday when data were scarce, but leads to data overload and information blackout now that they are plentiful. Or they believe that information specialists know what data executives and professionals need in order to have information. But information specialists are tool makers. They can tell us what tool to use to hammer upholstery nails into a chair. We need to decide whether we should be upholstering a chair at all.

Executives and professional specialists need to think through what information is for them, what data they need: first, to know what they are doing; then, to be able to decide what they should be doing; and finally, to appraise how well they are doing. Until this happens MIS departments are likely to remain cost centers rather than become the result centers they could be.

Most large businesses have little in common with the examples we have been looking at. Yet to remain competitive—maybe even to survive—they will have to convert themselves into information-based organizations, and fairly quickly. They will have to change old habits and acquire new ones. And the more successful a company has been, the more difficult and painful this process is apt to be. It will threaten the jobs, status, and opportunities of a good many people in the organization, especially the long-serving, middle-aged people in middle management who tend to be the least mobile and to feel most secure in their work, their positions, their relationships, and their behavior.

The information-based organization will also pose its own special management problems. I see as particularly critical:

1. Developing rewards, recognition, and career opportunities for specialists.
2. Creating unified vision in an organization of specialists.
3. Devising the management structure for an organization of task forces.
4. Ensuring the supply, preparation, and testing of top management people.

Bassoonists presumably neither want nor expect to be anything but bassoonists. Their career opportunities consist of moving from second bassoon to first bassoon and perhaps of moving from a second-rank orchestra to a better, more prestigious one. Similarly, many medical technologists neither expect nor want to be anything but medical technologists. Their career opportunities consist of a fairly good chance of moving up to senior technician, and a very slim chance of becoming lab director. For those who make it to lab director, about 1 out of every 25 or 30 technicians, there is also the opportunity to move to a bigger, richer hospital. The district officer in India had practically no chance for professional growth except possibly to be relocated, after a three-year stint, to a bigger district.

Opportunities for specialists in an information-based business organization should be more plentiful than they are in an orchestra or hospital, let alone in the Indian civil service. But as in these organizations, they will primarily be opportunities for advancement

> *To remain competitive—maybe even to survive—businesses will have to convert themselves into organizations of knowledgeable specialists.*

within the specialty, and for limited advancement at that. Advancement into "management" will be the exception, for the simple reason that there will be far fewer middle-management positions to move into. This contrasts sharply with the traditional organization where, except in the research lab, the main line of advancement in rank is out of the specialty and into general management.

More than 30 years ago General Electric tackled this problem by creating "parallel opportunities" for "individual professional contributors." Many companies have followed this example. But professional specialists themselves have largely rejected it as a solution. To them – and to their management colleagues – the only meaningful opportunities are promotions into management. And the prevailing compensation structure in practically all businesses reinforces this attitude because it is heavily biased towards managerial positions and titles.

There are no easy answers to this problem. Some help may come from looking at large law and consulting firms, where even the most senior partners tend to be specialists, and associates who will not make partner are outplaced fairly early on. But whatever scheme is eventually developed will work only if the values and compensation structure of business are drastically changed.

The second challenge that management faces is giving its organization of specialists a common vision, a view of the whole.

In the Indian civil service, the district officer was expected to see the "whole" of his district. But to enable him to concentrate on it, the government services that arose one after the other in the nineteenth century (forestry, irrigation, the archaeological survey, public health and sanitation, roads) were organized outside the administrative structure, and had virtually no contact with the district officer. This meant that the district officer became increasingly isolated from the activities that often had the greatest impact on – and the greatest importance for – his district. In the end, only the provincial government or the central government in Delhi had a view of the "whole," and it was an increasingly abstract one at that.

A business simply cannot function this way. It needs a view of the whole and a focus on the whole to be shared among a great many of its professional specialists, certainly among the senior ones. And yet it will have to accept, indeed will have to foster, the pride and professionalism of its specialists – if only because, in the absence of opportunities to move into middle management, their motivation must come from that pride and professionalism.

One way to foster professionalism, of course, is through assignments to task forces. And the information-based business will use more and more smaller self-governing units, assigning them tasks tidy enough for "a good man to get his arms around," as the old phrase has it. But to what extent should information-based businesses rotate performing specialists out of their specialties and into new ones? And to what extent will top management have to accept as its top priority making and maintaining a common vision across professional specialties?

Heavy reliance on task-force teams assuages one problem. But it aggravates another: the management structure of the information-based organization. Who will the business's managers be? Will they be task-force leaders? Or will there be a two-headed monster – a specialist structure, comparable, perhaps, to the way attending physi-

Who will the business's managers be?

cians function in a hospital, and an administrative structure of task-force leaders?

The decisions we face on the role and function of the task-force leaders are risky and controversial. Is theirs a permanent assignment, analogous to the job of the supervisory nurse in the hospital? Or is it a function of the task that changes as the task does? Is it an assignment or a position? Does it carry any rank at all? And if it does, will the task-force leaders become in time what the product managers have been at Procter & Gamble: the basic units of management and the company's field officers? Might the task-force leaders eventually replace department heads and vice presidents?

Signs of every one of these developments exist, but there is neither a clear trend nor much understanding as to what each entails. Yet each would give rise to a different organizational structure from any we are familiar with.

Finally, the toughest problem will probably be to ensure the supply, preparation, and testing of top management people. This is, of course, an old and central dilemma as well as a major reason for the general acceptance of decentralization in large businesses in the last 40 years. But the existing business organization has a great many middle-management positions that are supposed to prepare and test a person. As a result, there are usually a good many people to choose from when filling a senior management slot. With the number of middle-management positions sharply cut, where will the information-based organization's top executives come from? What will be their preparation? How will they have been tested?

With middle management sharply cut, where will the top executives come from?

Decentralization into autonomous units will surely be even more critical than it is now. Perhaps we will even copy the German *Gruppe* in which the decentralized units are set up as separate companies with their own top managements. The Germans use this model precisely because of their tradition of promoting people in their specialties, especially in research and engineering; if they did not have available commands in near-independent subsidiaries to put people in, they would have little opportunity to train and test their most promising professionals. These subsidiaries are thus somewhat like the farm teams of a major-league baseball club.

We may also find that more and more top management jobs in big companies are filled by hiring people away from smaller companies. This is the way that major orchestras get their conductors—a young conductor earns his or her spurs in a small orchestra or opera house, only to be hired away by a larger one. And the heads of a good many large hospitals have had similar careers.

Can business follow the example of the orchestra and hospital where top management has become a separate career? Conductors and hospital administrators come out of courses in conducting or schools of hospital administration respectively. We see something of this sort in France, where large companies are often run by men who have spent their entire previous careers in government service. But in most countries this would be unacceptable to the organization (only France has the *mystique* of the *grandes écoles*). And even in France, businesses, especially large ones, are becoming too demanding to be run by people without firsthand experience and a proven success record.

Thus the entire top management process—preparation, testing, succession—will become even more problematic than it already is.

There will be a growing need for experienced businesspeople to go back to school. And business schools will surely need to work out what successful professional specialists must know to prepare themselves for high-level positions as *business* executives and *business* leaders.

Since modern business enterprise first arose, after the Civil War in the United States and the Franco-Prussian War in Europe, there have been two major evolutions in the concept and structure of organizations. The first took place in the ten years between 1895 and 1905. It distinguished management from ownership and established management as work and task in its own right. This happened first in Germany, when Georg Siemens, the founder and head of Germany's premier bank, *Deutsche Bank*, saved the electrical apparatus company his cousin Werner had founded after Werner's sons and heirs had mismanaged it into near collapse. By threatening to cut off the bank's loans, he forced his cousins to turn the company's management over to professionals. A little later, J.P. Morgan, Andrew Carnegie, and John D. Rockefeller, Sr. followed suit in their massive restructurings of U.S. railroads and industries.

The second evolutionary change took place 20 years later. The development of what we still see as the modern corporation began with Pierre S. du Pont's restructuring of his family company in the early twenties and continued with Alfred P. Sloan's redesign of General Motors a few years later. This introduced the command-and-control organization of today, with its emphasis on decentralization, central service staffs, personnel management, the whole apparatus of budgets and controls, and the important distinction between policy and operations. This stage culminated in the massive reorganization of General Electric in the early 1950s, an action that perfected the model most big businesses around the world (including Japanese organizations) still follow.[2]

Now we are entering a third period of change: the shift from the command-and-control organization, the organization of departments and divisions, to the information-based organization, the organization of knowledge specialists. We can perceive, though perhaps only dimly, what this organization will look like. We can identify some of its main characteristics and requirements. We can point to central problems of values, structure, and behavior. But the job of actually building the information-based organization is still ahead of us – it is the managerial challenge of the future.

We can identify requirements and point to problems; the job of building is still ahead.

Reprint 88105

---

2. Alfred D. Chandler, Jr. has masterfully chronicled the process in his two books *Strategy and Structure* (Cambridge: MIT Press, 1962) and *The Visible Hand* (Cambridge: Harvard University Press, 1977) – surely the best studies of the administrative history of any major institution. The process itself and its results were presented and analyzed in two of my books: *The Concept of the Corporation* (New York: John Day, 1946) and *The Practice of Management* (New York: Harper Brothers, 1954).

People are the key to managing complex strategies and organizations.

Matrix Management: Not a Structure, a Frame of Mind

by Christopher A. Bartlett and Sumantra Ghoshal

Top-level managers in many of today's leading corporations are losing control of their companies. The problem is not that they have misjudged the demands created by an increasingly complex environment and an accelerating rate of environmental change, nor even that they have failed to develop strategies appropriate to the new challenges. The problem is that their companies are organizationally incapable of carrying out the sophisticated strategies they have developed. Over the past 20 years, strategic thinking has far outdistanced organizational capabilities.

All through the 1980s, companies everywhere were redefining their strategies and reconfiguring their operations in response to such developments as the globalization of markets, the intensification of competition, the acceleration of product life cycles, and the growing complexity of relationships with suppliers, customers, employees, governments, even competitors. But as companies struggled with these changing environmental realities, many fell into one of two traps—one strategic, one structural.

The strategic trap was to implement simple, static solutions to complex and dynamic problems. The bait was often a consultant's siren song promising to simplify or at least minimize complexity and discontinuity. Despite the new demands of overlapping industry boundaries and greatly altered value-added chains, managers were promised success if they would "stick to their knitting"; in a swiftly changing international political economy, they were urged to rein in dispersed overseas operations and focus on the "triad markets"; and in an increasingly intricate and sophisticated competitive environment, they were encouraged to choose between alternative "generic strategies"—low cost or differentiation.

Yet the strategic reality for most companies was that both their business and their environment really *were* more complex, while the proposed solutions were often simple, even simplistic. The traditional telephone company that stuck to its knitting was trampled by competitors who redefined their strategies in response to new technologies linking telecommunications, computers, and office equipment into a single integrated system. The packaged-goods company that concentrated on the triad markets quickly discovered that Europe, Japan, and the United States were the epicenters of global competitive activity, with higher risks and slimmer profits than more protected and less competitive markets like Australia, Turkey, and Brazil. The consumer electronics company that adopted an either-or generic strategy found itself facing competitors able to develop cost and differentiation capabilities at the same time.

In recent years, as more and more managers recognized oversimplification as a strategic trap, they began to accept the need to manage complexity rather than seek to minimize it. This realization, however, led many into an equally threatening organizational trap when they concluded that the best response to increasingly complex strategic requirements was increasingly complex organizational structures.

The obvious organizational solution to strategies that required multiple, simultaneous management capabilities was the matrix structure that became so fashionable in the late 1970s and the early 1980s. Its parallel reporting relationships acknowledged the diverse, conflicting needs of functional, product, and geographic management groups and provided a formal mechanism for resolving them. Its multiple information channels allowed the organization to capture and analyze external complexity. And its overlapping responsibilities were designed to combat parochialism and build flexibility into the company's response to change.

In practice, however, the matrix proved all but unmanageable—especially in an international context. Dual reporting led to conflict and confusion; the proliferation of channels created informational logjams as a proliferation of committees and reports

> **The CEO as strategic guru is a thing of the past. CEOs must now focus on finding and motivating talent.**

bogged down the organization; and overlapping responsibilities produced turf battles and a loss of accountability. Separated by barriers of distance, language, time, and culture, managers found it virtually impossible to clarify the confusion and resolve the conflicts.

In hindsight, the strategic and structural traps seem simple enough to avoid, so one has to wonder why so many experienced general managers have fallen into them. Much of the answer lies in the way we have traditionally thought about the general manager's role. For decades, we have seen the general manager as chief strategic guru and principal organizational architect. But as the competitive climate grows less stable and less predictable, it is harder for one person alone to succeed in that great visionary role. Similarly, as formal, hierarchical structure gives way to networks of personal relationships that work through informal, horizontal communication channels, the image of top management in an isolated corner office moving boxes and lines on an organization chart becomes increasingly anachronistic.

Paradoxically, as strategies and organizations become more complex and sophisticated, top-level general managers are beginning to replace their historical concentration on the grand issues of strategy and structure with a focus on the details of managing people and processes. The critical strategic requirement is not to devise the most ingenious and well

---

Christopher A. Bartlett is a professor of general management at the Harvard Business School, where he is also chairman of the International Senior Management program. Sumantra Ghoshal is an associate professor who teaches business policy at the European Institute of Business Administration (INSEAD) in Fontainebleau, France. This article is based on a research project reported in detail in their recent book, Managing Across Borders: The Transnational Solution *(Harvard Business School Press, 1989).*

coordinated plan but to build the most viable and flexible strategic process; the key organizational task is not to design the most elegant structure but to capture individual capabilities and motivate the entire organization to respond cooperatively to a complicated and dynamic environment.

Building an Organization

While business thinkers have written a great deal about strategic innovation, they have paid far less attention to the accompanying organizational challenges. Yet many companies remain caught in the structural-complexity trap that paralyzes their ability to respond quickly or flexibly to the new strategic imperatives.

For those companies that adopted matrix structures, the problem was not in the way they defined the goal. They correctly recognized the need for a multidimensional organization to respond to growing external complexity. The problem was that they defined their organizational objectives in purely structural terms. Yet formal structure describes only the organization's basic anatomy. Companies must also concern themselves with organizational physiology—the systems and relationships that allow the lifeblood of information to flow through the organization. And they need to develop a healthy organizational psychology—the shared norms, values, and beliefs that shape the way individual managers think and act.

The companies that fell into the organizational trap assumed that changing their formal structure (anatomy) would force changes in interpersonal relationships and decision processes (physiology), which in turn would reshape the individual attitudes and actions of managers (psychology).

But as many companies have discovered, reconfiguring the formal structure is a blunt and sometimes brutal instrument of change. A new structure creates new and presumably more useful managerial ties, but these can take months and often years to evolve into effective knowledge-generating and decision-making relationships. And since the new job requirements will frustrate, alienate, or simply overwhelm so many managers, changes in individual attitudes and behavior will likely take even longer.

As companies struggle to create organizational capabilities that reflect rather than diminish environmental complexity, good managers gradually stop searching for the ideal structural template to impose on the company from the top down. Instead, they focus on the challenge of building up an appropriate set of employee attitudes and skills and linking them together with carefully developed processes and relationships. In other words, they begin to focus on building the organization rather than simply on installing a new structure.

Indeed, the companies that are most successful at developing multidimensional organizations begin at the far end of the anatomy-physiology-psychology sequence. Their first objective is to alter the organizational psychology—the broad corporate beliefs and norms that shape managers' perceptions and actions. Then, by enriching and clarifying communication and decision processes, companies reinforce these psychological changes with improvements in organizational physiology. Only later do they consolidate and confirm their progress by realigning organizational anatomy through changes in the formal structure.

No company we know of has discovered a quick or easy way to change its organizational psychology to reshape the understanding, identification, and commitment of its employees. But we found three principal characteristics common to those that managed the task most effectively:

1. The development and communication of a clear and consistent corporate vision.

2. The effective management of human resource tools to broaden individual perspectives and develop identification with corporate goals.

3. The integration of individual thinking and activities into the broad corporate agenda by means of a process we call co-option.

Building a Shared Vision

Perhaps the main reason managers in large, complex companies cling to parochial attitudes is that their frame of reference is bounded by their specific responsibilities. The surest way to break down such insularity is to develop and communicate a clear sense of corporate purpose that extends into every corner of the company and gives context and meaning to each manager's particular roles and responsibilities. We are not talking about a slogan, however catchy and pointed. We are talking about a company vision, which must be crafted and articulated with clarity, continuity, and consistency: clarity of expression that makes company objectives understandable and meaningful; continuity of purpose that underscores their enduring importance; and consistency of application across business units and geographical boundaries that ensures uniformity throughout the organization.

Clarity. There are three keys to clarity in a corporate vision: simplicity, relevance, and reinforcement. NEC's integration of computers and communications–C&C–is probably the best single example of how simplicity can make a vision more powerful. Top management has applied the C&C concept so effectively that it describes the company's business focus, defines its distinctive source of competitive advantage over large companies like IBM and AT&T, and summarizes its strategic and organizational imperatives.

The second key, relevance, means linking broad objectives to concrete agendas. When Wisse Dekker became CEO at Philips, his principal strategic concern was the problem of competing with Japan. He stated this challenge in martial terms–the U.S. had abandoned the battlefield; Philips was now Europe's last defense against insurgent Japanese electronics companies. By focusing the company's attention not only on Philips's corporate survival but also on the protection of national and regional interests, Dekker heightened the sense of urgency and commitment in a way that legitimized cost-cutting efforts, drove an extensive rationalization of plant operations, and inspired a new level of sales achievements.

The third key to clarity is top management's continual reinforcement, elaboration, and interpretation of the core vision to keep it from becoming obsolete or abstract. Founder Konosuke Matsushita developed a grand, 250-year vision for his company, but he also managed to give it immediate relevance. He summed up its overall message in the "Seven Spirits of Matsushita," to which he referred constantly in his policy statements. Each January he wove the company's one-year operational objectives into his overarching concept to produce an annual theme that he then captured in a slogan. For all the loftiness of his concept of corporate purpose, he gave his managers immediate, concrete guidance in implementing Matsushita's goals.

Continuity. Despite shifts in leadership and continual adjustments in short-term business priorities, companies must remain committed to the same core set of strategic objectives and organizational values. Without such continuity, unifying vision might as well be expressed in terms of quarterly goals.

It was General Electric's lack of this kind of continuity that led to the erosion of its once formidable position in electrical appliances in many countries. Over a period of 20 years and under successive CEOs, the company's international consumer-product strategy never stayed the same for long. From building locally responsive and self-sufficient "mini-GEs" in each market, the company turned to a policy of developing low-cost offshore sources, which eventually evolved into a de facto strategy of international outsourcing. Finally, following its acquisition of RCA, GE's consumer electronics strategy made another about-face and focused on building centralized scale to defend domestic share. Meanwhile, the product strategy within this shifting business emphasis was itself unstable. The Brazilian subsidiary, for example, built its TV business in the 1960s until it was told to stop; in the early 1970s, it emphasized large appliances until it was denied funding; then it focused on housewares until the parent company sold off that business. In two decades, GE utterly dissipated its dominant franchise in Brazil's electrical products market.

Unilever, by contrast, made an enduring commitment to its Brazilian subsidiary, despite volatile swings in Brazil's business climate. Company chairman Floris Maljers emphasized the importance of

> **In a mere 20 years, GE squandered its dominant place in Brazil's electrical products market.**

looking past the latest political crisis or economic downturn to the long-term business potential. "In those parts of the world," he remarked, "you take your management cues from the way they dance. The samba method of management is two steps forward then one step back." Unilever built–two steps forward and one step back–a profitable $300 million business in a rapidly growing economy with 130 million consumers, while its wallflower competitors never ventured out onto the floor.

Consistency. The third task for top management in communicating strategic purpose is to ensure that everyone in the company shares the same vision. The cost of inconsistency can be horrendous. It always produces confusion and, in extreme cases, can lead to total chaos, with different units of the organization pursuing agendas that are mutually debilitating.

Philips is a good example of a company that, for a time, lost its consistency of corporate purpose. As a legacy of its wartime decision to give some overseas units legal autonomy, management had long experienced difficulty persuading North American Philips (NAP) to play a supportive role in the parent company's global strategies. The problem came to a head with the introduction of Philips's technologically first-rate videocassette recording system, the V2000. Despite considerable pressure from world headquarters in the Netherlands, NAP refused to launch the system, arguing that Sony's Beta system and Matsushita's VHS format were too well established and had cost, feature, and system-support advantages Philips couldn't match. Relying on its legal independence and managerial autonomy, NAP management decided instead to source products from its Japanese competitors and market them under its Magnavox brand name. As a result, Philips was unable to build the efficiency and credibility it needed to challenge Japanese dominance of the VCR business.

Most inconsistencies involve differences between what managers of different operating units see as the company's key objectives. Sometimes, however, different corporate leaders transmit different views of overall priorities and purpose. When this stems from poor communication, it can be fixed. When it's a result of fundamental disagreement, the problem is serious indeed, as illustrated by ITT's problems in developing its strategically vital System 12 switching equipment. Continuing differences between the head of the European organization and the company's chief technology officer over the location and philosophy of the development effort led to confusion and conflict throughout the company. The result was disastrous. ITT had difficulty transferring vital technology across its own unit boundaries and so was irreparably late introducing this key product to a rapidly changing global market. These problems eventually led the company to sell off its core telecommunications business to a competitor.

But formulating and communicating a vision–no matter how clear, enduring, and consistent–cannot succeed unless individual employees understand and accept the company's stated goals and objectives. Problems at this level are more often related to receptivity than to communication. The development of individual understanding and acceptance is a challenge for a company's human resource practices.

Developing Human Resources

While top managers universally recognize their responsibility for developing and allocating a company's scarce assets and resources, their focus on finance and technology often overshadows the task of developing the scarcest resource of all–capable managers. But if there is one key to regaining control of companies that operate in fast-changing environments, it is the ability of top management to turn the perceptions, capabilities, and relationships of individual managers into the building blocks of the organization.

One pervasive problem in companies whose leaders lack this ability–or fail to exercise it–is getting managers to see how their specific responsibilities relate to the broad corporate vision. Growing external complexity and strategic sophistication have accelerated the growth of a cadre of specialists who are physically and organizationally isolated from each other, and the task of dealing with their consequent parochialism should not be delegated to the

> Global coordination failed at ITT, where each national company was an independent fiefdom.

clerical staff that administers salary structures and benefit programs. Top managers inside and outside the human resource function must be leaders in the recruitment, development, and assignment of the company's vital human talent.

Recruitment and Selection. The first step in successfully managing complexity is to tap the full range of available talent. It is a serious mistake to permit historical imbalances in the nationality or functional background of the management group to constrain hiring or subsequent promotion. In today's global marketplace, domestically oriented recruiting limits a company's ability to capitalize on its worldwide pool of management skill and biases its decision-making processes.

After decades of routinely appointing managers from its domestic operations to key positions in overseas subsidiaries, Procter & Gamble realized that the practice not only worked against sensitivity to local cultures–a lesson driven home by several marketing failures in Japan–but also greatly underutilized its pool of high-potential non-American managers. (Fortunately, our studies turned up few companies as shortsighted as one that made overseas assignments on the basis of *poor* performance, since foreign markets were assumed to be "not as tough as the domestic environment.")

Not only must companies enlarge the pool of people available for key positions, they must also develop new criteria for choosing those most likely to succeed. Because past success is no longer a sufficient qualification for increasingly subtle, sensitive, and unpredictable senior-level tasks, top management must become involved in a more discriminating selection process. At Matsushita, top management selects candidates for international assignment on the basis of a comprehensive set of personal characteristics, expressed for simplicity in the acronym SMILE: specialty (the needed skill, capability, or knowledge); management ability (particularly motivational ability); international flexibility (willingness to learn and ability to adapt); language facility; and endeavor (vitality, perseverance in the face of difficulty). These attributes are remarkably similar to those targeted by NEC and Philips, where top executives also are involved in the senior-level selection process.

Training and Development. Once the appropriate top-level candidates have been identified, the next challenge is to develop their potential. The most successful development efforts have three aims that take them well beyond the skill-building objectives of classic training programs: to inculcate a common vision and shared values; to broaden management perspectives and capabilities; and to develop contacts and shape management relationships.

To build common vision and values, white-collar employees at Matsushita spend a good part of their first six months in what the company calls "cultural and spiritual training." They study the company credo, the "Seven Spirits of Matsushita," and the philosophy of Konosuke Matsushita. Then they learn how to translate these internalized lessons into daily behavior and even operational decisions. Culture-building exercises as intensive as Matsushita's are sometimes dismissed as the kind of Japanese mumbo jumbo that would not work in other societies, but in fact, Philips has a similar entry-level training practice (called "organization cohesion training"), as does Unilever (called, straightforwardly, "indoctrination").

The second objective—broadening management perspectives—is essentially a matter of teaching people how to manage complexity instead of merely to make room for it. To reverse a long and unwieldy tradition of running its operations with two- and three-headed management teams of separate technical, commercial, and sometimes administrative specialists, Philips asked its training and development group to de-specialize top management trainees. By supplementing its traditional menu of specialist courses and functional programs with more intensive general management training, Philips was able to begin replacing the ubiquitous teams with single business heads who also appreciated and respected specialist points of view.

The final aim—developing contacts and relationships—is much more than an incidental by-product of good management development, as the comments of a senior personnel manager at Unilever suggest: "By bringing managers from different countries and businesses together at Four Acres [Unilever's international management training college], we build contacts and create bonds that we could never achieve by other means. The company spends as much on training as it does on R&D not only because of the direct effect it has on upgrading skills and knowledge but also because it plays a central role in indoctrinating managers into a Unilever club where personal relationships and informal contacts are much more powerful than the formal systems and structures."

Career-Path Management. Although recruitment and training are critically important, the most effective companies recognize that the best way to develop new perspectives and thwart parochialism in their managers is through personal experience. By moving selected managers across functions, businesses, and geographic units, a company encourages cross-fertilization of ideas as well as the flexibility and breadth of experience that enable managers to grapple with complexity and come out on top.

Unilever has long been committed to the development of its human resources as a means of attaining durable competitive advantage. As early as the 1930s, the company was recruiting and developing local employees to replace the parent-company managers who had been running most of its overseas subsidiaries. In a practice that came to be known as "-ization," the company committed itself to the Indianization of its Indian company, the Australization of its Australian company, and so on.

Although delighted with the new talent that began working its way up through the organization, management soon realized that by reducing the transfer

> **Unilever has so Unileverized its managers that they can spot one another anywhere in the world.**

of parent-company managers abroad, it had diluted the powerful glue that bound diverse organizational groups together and linked dispersed operations. The answer lay in formalizing a second phase of the -ization process. While continuing with Indianization, for example, Unilever added programs aimed at the Unileverization of its Indian managers.

In addition to bringing 300 to 400 managers to Four Acres each year, Unilever typically has 100 to 150 of its most promising overseas managers on short- and long-term job assignments at corporate headquarters. This policy not only brings fresh, close-to-the-market perspectives into corporate decision making but also gives the visiting managers a strong sense of Unilever's strategic vision and organizational values. In the words of one of the expatriates in the corporate offices, "The experience initiates you into the Unilever Club and the clear norms, values, and behaviors that distinguish our people—so much so that we really believe we can spot another Unilever manager anywhere in the world."

Furthermore, the company carefully transfers most of these high-potential individuals through a variety of different functional, product, and geographic positions, often rotating every two or three years. Most important, top management tracks about 1,000 of these people—some 5% of Unilever's total management group—who, as they move through the company, forge an informal network of contacts and relationships that is central to Unilever's decision-making and information-exchange processes.

Widening the perspectives and relationships of key managers as Unilever has done is a good way of developing identification with the broader corporate mission. But a broad sense of identity is not enough. To maintain control of its global strategies, Unilever must secure a strong and lasting individual commitment to corporate visions and objectives. In effect, it must co-opt individual energies and ambitions into the service of corporate goals.

Co-Opting Management Efforts

As organizational complexity grows, managers and management groups tend to become so specialized and isolated and to focus so intently on their own immediate operating responsibilities that they are apt to respond parochially to intrusions on their organizational turf, even when the overall corporate interest is at stake. A classic example, described earlier, was the decision by North American Philips's consumer electronics group to reject the parent company's VCR system.

At about the same time, Philips, like many other companies, began experimenting with ways to convert managers' intellectual understanding of the corporate vision—in Philips's case, an almost evangelical determination to defend Western electronics against the Japanese—into a binding personal commitment. Philips concluded that it could co-opt individuals and organizational groups into the broader vision by inviting them to contribute to the corporate agenda and then giving them direct responsibility for implementation.

In the face of intensifying Japanese competition, Philips knew it had to improve coordination in its consumer electronics among its fiercely independent national organizations. In strengthening the central product divisions, however, Philips did not want to deplete the enterprise or commitment of its capable national management teams.

The company met these conflicting needs with two cross-border initiatives. First, it created a top-level World Policy Council for its video business that included key managers from strategic markets—Germany, France, the United Kingdom, the United States, and Japan. Philips knew that its national companies' long history of independence made local managers reluctant to take orders from Dutch headquarters in Eindhoven—often for good reason, since much of the company's best market knowledge and technological expertise resided in its offshore units. Through the council, Philips co-opted their support for company decisions about product policy and manufacturing location.

Second, and more powerful, Philips allocated global responsibilities to units that had previously been purely national in focus. Eindhoven gave NAP the leading role in the development of Philips's projection television and asked it to coordinate development and manufacture of all Philips television sets for North America and Asia. The change in the attitude of NAP managers was dramatic.

A senior manager in NAP's consumer electronics business summed up the feelings of U.S. managers: "At last, we are moving out of the dependency relationship with Eindhoven that was so frustrating to us." Co-option had transformed the defensive, territorial attitude of NAP managers into a more collaborative mind-set. They were making important contributions to global corporate strategy instead of looking for ways to subvert it.

In 1987, with much of its TV set production established in Mexico, the president of NAP's consumer electronics group told the press, "It is the commonality of design that makes it possible for us to move production globally. We have splendid cooperation with Philips in Eindhoven." It was a statement no NAP manager would have made a few years earlier, and it perfectly captured how effectively Philips had co-opted previously isolated, even adversarial, managers into the corporate agenda.

The Matrix in the Manager's Mind

Since the end of World War II, corporate strategy has survived several generations of painful transformation and has grown appropriately agile and athletic. Unfortunately, organizational development has not kept pace, and managerial attitudes lag even further behind. As a result, corporations now commonly design strategies that seem impossible to implement, for the simple reason that no one can effectively implement third-generation strategies through second-generation organizations run by first-generation managers.

Today the most successful companies are those where top executives recognize the need to manage the new environmental and competitive demands by focusing less on the quest for an ideal structure and more on developing the abilities, behavior, and performance of individual managers. Change succeeds only when those assigned to the new transnational and interdependent tasks understand the overall goals and are dedicated to achieving them.

One senior executive put it this way: "The challenge is not so much to build a matrix structure as it is to create a matrix in the minds of our managers." The inbuilt conflict in a matrix structure pulls managers in several directions at once. Developing a matrix of flexible perspectives and relationships within each manager's mind, however, achieves an entirely different result. It lets individuals make the judgments and negotiate the trade-offs that drive the organization toward a shared strategic objective.

Reprint 90401

"We're immortals and all that, but quite a few of us are locked into some very stupid, dead-end jobs."

The New Managerial Work

by Rosabeth Moss Kanter

Managerial work is undergoing such enormous and rapid change that many managers are reinventing their profession as they go. With little precedent to guide them, they are watching hierarchy fade away and the clear distinctions of title, task, department, even corporation, blur. Faced with extraordinary levels of complexity and interdependency, they watch traditional sources of power erode and the old motivational tools lose their magic.

The cause is obvious. Competitive pressures are forcing corporations to adopt new flexible strategies and structures. Many of these are familiar: acquisitions and divestitures aimed at more focused combinations of business activities, reductions in management staff and levels of hierarchy, increased use of performance-based rewards. Other strategies are less common but have an even more profound effect. In a growing number of companies, for example, horizontal ties between peers are replacing vertical ties as channels of activity and communication. Companies are asking corporate staffs and functional departments to play a more strategic role with greater cross-departmental collaboration. Some organizations are turning themselves nearly inside out — buying formerly internal services from outside suppliers, forming strategic alliances and supplier-customer partnerships that bring external relationships inside where they can influence company policy and practice. I call these emerging practices "postentrepreneurial" because they involve the application of entrepreneurial creativity and flexibility to established businesses.

Such changes come highly recommended by the experts who urge organizations to become leaner, less bureaucratic, more entrepreneurial. But so far, theorists have given scant attention to the dramatically altered realities of managerial work in these transformed corporations. We don't even have good words to describe the new relationships. "Superiors" and "subordinates" hardly seem accurate, and even "bosses" and "their people" imply more control and ownership than managers today actually possess. On top of it all, career paths are no longer straightforward and predictable but have become idiosyncratic and confusing.

Some managers experience the new managerial work as a loss of power because much of their authority used to come from hierarchical position. Now that everything seems negotiable by everyone, they are confused about how to mobilize and motivate staff. For other managers, the shift in roles and tasks offers greater personal power. The following case histories illustrate the responses of three managers in

Rosabeth Moss Kanter holds the Class of 1960 Chair as Professor of Business Administration at the Harvard Business School and concentrates on innovation and entrepreneurship in established companies. Her most recent book is When Giants Learn to Dance: Mastering the Challenges of Strategy, Management, and Careers in the 1990s *(Simon & Schuster, 1989).*

The New Managerial Quandaries

■ At American Express, the CEO instituted a program called "One Enterprise" to encourage collaboration between different lines of business. One Enterprise has led to a range of projects where peers from different divisions work together on such synergistic ventures as cross-marketing, joint purchasing, and cooperative product and market innovation. Employees' rewards are tied to their One Enterprise efforts. Executives set goals and can earn bonuses for their contributions to results in other divisions.
☐ But how do department managers control their people when they're working on cross-departmental teams? And who determines the size of the rewards when the interests of more than one area are involved?

■ At Security Pacific National Bank, internal departments have become forces in the external marketplace. For example, the bank is involved in a joint venture with local auto dealers to sell fast financing for car purchases. And the MIS department is now a profit center selling its services inside and outside the bank.
☐ But what is the role of bank managers accountable for the success of such entrepreneurial ventures? And how do they shift their orientation from the role of boss in a chain of command to the role of customer?

■ At Digital Equipment Corporation, emphasis on supplier partnerships to improve quality and innovation has multiplied the need for cross-functional as well as cross-company collaboration. Key suppliers are included on product planning teams with engineering, manufacturing, and purchasing staff. Digital uses its human resources staff to train and do performance appraisals of its suppliers, as if they were part of the company. In cases where suppliers are also customers, purchasing and marketing departments also need to work collaboratively.
☐ But how do managers learn enough about other functions to be credible, let alone influential, members of such teams? How do they maintain adequate communication externally while staying on top of what their own departments are doing? And how do they handle the extra work of responding to projects initiated by other areas?

■ At Banc One, a growing reliance on project teams spanning more than 70 affiliated banks has led the CEO to propose eliminating officer titles because of the lack of correlation between status as measured by title and status within the collaborative team.
☐ But then what do "rank" and "hierarchy" mean anymore, especially for people whose careers consist of a sequence of projects rather than a sequence of promotions? What does "career" mean? Does it have a shape? Is there a ladder?

■ At Alcan, which is trying to find new uses and applications for its core product, aluminum, managers and professionals from line divisions form screening teams to consider and refine new-venture proposals. A venture manager, chosen from the screening team, takes charge of concepts that pass muster, drawing on Alcan's worldwide resources to build the new business. In one case of global synergy, Alcan created a new product for the Japanese market using Swedish and American technology and Canadian manufacturing capacity.
☐ But why should senior managers release staff to serve on screening and project teams for new businesses when their own businesses are making do with fewer and fewer people? How do functionally oriented managers learn enough about worldwide developments to know when they might have something of value to offer someplace else? And how do the managers of these new ventures ever go back to the conventional line organization as middle managers once their venture has been folded into an established division?

■ At IBM, an emphasis on customer partnerships to rebuild market share is leading to practices quite new to the company. In some cases, IBM has formed joint development teams with customers, where engineers from both companies share proprietary data. In others, the company has gone beyond selling equipment to actually managing a customer's management information system. Eastman Kodak has handed its U.S. data center operations to IBM to consolidate and manage, which means lower fixed costs for Kodak and a greater ability to focus on its core businesses rather than on ancillary services. Some 300 former Kodak people still fill Kodak's needs as IBM employees, while two committees of IBM and Kodak managers oversee the partnership.
☐ But who exactly do the data center people work for? Who is in charge? And how do traditional notions of managerial authority square with such a complicated set of relationships?

three different industries to the opportunities and dilemmas of structural change.

Hank is vice president and chief engineer for a leading heavy equipment manufacturer that is moving aggressively against foreign competition. One of the company's top priorities has been to increase the speed, quality, and cost-effectiveness of product development. So Hank worked with consultants to improve collaboration between manufacturing and other functions and to create closer alliances between the company and its outside suppliers. Gradually, a highly segmented operation became an integrated process involving project teams drawn from component divisions, functional departments, and external suppliers. But along the way, there were several unusual side effects. Different areas of responsibility overlapped. Some technical and manufacturing people were co-located. Liaisons from functional areas joined the larger development teams. Most unusual of all, project teams had a lot of direct contact with higher levels of the company.

Many of the managers reporting to Hank felt these changes as a loss of power. They didn't always know what their people were doing, but they still believed they ought to know. They no longer had sole input into performance appraisals; other people from other

> **New strategies challenge the old power of managers and shake hierarchy to its roots.**

functions had a voice as well, and some of them knew more about employees' project performance. New career paths made it less important to please direct superiors in order to move up the functional line.

Moreover, employees often bypassed Hank's managers and interacted directly with decision makers inside and outside the company. Some of these so-called subordinates had contact with division executives and senior corporate staff, and sometimes they sat in on high-level strategy meetings to which their managers were not invited.

At first Hank thought his managers' resistance to the new process was just the normal noise associated with any change. Then he began to realize that something more profound was going on. The reorganization was challenging traditional notions about the role and power of managers and shaking traditional hierarchy to its roots. And no one could see what was taking its place.

When George became head of a major corporate department in a large bank holding company, he thought he had arrived. His title and rank were unmistakable, and his department was responsible for determining product-line policy for hundreds of bank branches and the virtual clerks – in George's eyes – who managed them. George staffed his department with MBAs and promised them rapid promotion.

Then the sand seemed to shift beneath him. Losing market position for the first time in recent memory, the bank decided to emphasize direct customer service at the branches. The people George considered clerks began to depart from George's standard policies and to tailor their services to local market conditions. In many cases, they actually demanded services and responses from George's staff, and the results of their requests began to figure in performance reviews of George's department. George's people were spending more and more time in the field with branch managers, and the corporate personnel department was even trying to assign some of George's MBAs to branch and regional posts.

To complicate matters, the bank's strategy included a growing role for technology. George felt that because he had no direct control over the information systems department, he should not be held fully accountable for every facet of product design and implementation. But fully accountable he was. He had to deploy people to learn the new technology and figure out how to work with it. Furthermore, the bank was asking product departments like George's to find ways to link existing products or develop new ones that crossed traditional categories. So George's people were often away on cross-departmental teams just when he wanted them for some internal assignment.

Instead of presiding over a tidy empire the way his predecessor had, George presided over what looked to him like chaos. The bank said senior executives should be "leaders, not managers," but George didn't know what that meant, especially since he seemed to have lost control over his subordinates' assignments, activities, rewards, and careers. He resented his perceived loss of status.

The CEO tried to show him that good results achieved the new way would bring great monetary rewards, thanks to a performance-based bonus program that was gradually replacing more modest yearly raises. But the pressures on George were also greater, unlike anything he'd ever experienced.

For Sally, purchasing manager at an innovative computer company, a new organizational strategy was a gain rather than a loss, although it changed her relationship with the people reporting to her. Less than ten years out of college, she was hired as an analyst – a semiprofessional, semiclerical job – then promoted to a purchasing manager's job in a sleepy staff department. She didn't expect to go much further in what was then a well-established hierarchy. But after a shocking downturn, top management encouraged employees to rethink traditional ways of doing things. Sally's boss, the head of purchasing, suggested that "partnerships" with key suppliers might improve quality, speed innovation, and reduce costs.

Soon Sally's backwater was at the center of policymaking, and Sally began to help shape strategy. She organized meetings between her company's senior executives and supplier CEOs. She sent her staff to contribute supplier intelligence at company semi-

> In the new organization, it's hard to tell the managers from the nonmanagers.

nars on technical innovation, and she spent more of her own time with product designers and manufacturing planners. She led senior executives on a tour of supplier facilities, traveling with them in the corporate jet.

Because some suppliers were also important customers, Sally's staff began meeting frequently with marketing managers to share information and address joint problems. Sally and her group were now also acting as internal advocates for major suppliers. Furthermore, many of these external companies now contributed performance appraisals of Sally and her team, and their opinions weighed almost as heavily as those of her superiors.

As a result of the company's new direction, Sally felt more personal power and influence, and her ties to peers in other areas and to top management were stronger. But she no longer felt like a manager directing subordinates. Her staff had become a pool of resources deployed by many others besides Sally. She was exhilarated by her personal opportunities but not quite sure the people she managed should have the same freedom to choose their own assignments. After all, wasn't that a manager's prerogative?

Hank's, George's, and Sally's very different stories say much about the changing nature of managerial work. However hard it is for managers at the very top to remake strategy and structure, they themselves will probably retain their identity, status, and control. For the managers below them, structural change is often much harder. As work units become more participative and team oriented, and as professionals and knowledge workers become more prominent, the distinction between manager and nonmanager begins to erode.

To understand what managers must do to achieve results in the postentrepreneurial corporation, we need to look at the changing picture of how such companies operate. The picture has five elements:

1. There are a greater number and variety of channels for taking action and exerting influence.

2. Relationships of influence are shifting from the vertical to the horizontal, from chain of command to peer networks.

3. The distinction between managers and those managed is diminishing, especially in terms of information, control over assignments, and access to external relationships.

4. External relationships are increasingly important as sources of internal power and influence, even of career development.

5. As a result of the first four changes, career development has become less intelligible but also less circumscribed. There are fewer assured routes to success, which produces anxiety. At the same time, career paths are more open to innovation, which produces opportunity.

To help companies implement their competitive organizational strategies, managers must learn new ways to manage, confronting changes in their own bases of power and recognizing the need for new ways to motivate people.

The Bases of Power

The changes I've talked about can be scary for people like George and the managers reporting to Hank, who were trained to know their place, to follow orders, to let the company take care of their careers, to do things by the book. The book is gone. In the new corporation, managers have only themselves to count on for success. They must learn to operate without the crutch of hierarchy. Position, title, and authority are no longer adequate tools, not in a world where subordinates are encouraged to think for themselves and where managers have to work synergistically with other departments and even other companies. Success depends increasingly on tapping into sources of good ideas, on figuring out whose collaboration is needed to act on those ideas, on working with both to produce results. In short, the new managerial work implies very different ways of obtaining and using power.

The postentrepreneurial corporation is not only leaner and flatter, it also has many more channels for action. Cross-functional projects, business-unit joint ventures, labor-management forums, innovation funds that spawn activities outside mainstream budgets and reporting lines, strategic partnerships with suppliers or customers—these are all overlays on the traditional organization chart, strategic pathways that ignore the chain of command.

Their existence has several important implications. For one thing, they create more potential centers of power. As the ways to combine resources increase, the ability to command diminishes. Alternative paths of communication, resource access, and execution erode the authority of those in the nominal chain of command. In other words, the opportunity for greater speed and flexibility undermines hierarchy. As more and more strategic action takes place in these channels, the jobs that focus inward on particular departments decline in power.

As a result, the ability of managers to get things done depends more on the number of networks in which they're centrally involved than on their height in a hierarchy. Of course, power in any organization always has a network component, but rank and formal structure used to be more limiting. For example, access to information and the ability to get informal backing were often confined to the few officially sanctioned contact points between departments or between the company and its vendors or customers. Today these official barriers are disappearing, while so-called informal networks grow in importance.

In the emerging organization, managers add value by deal making, by brokering at interfaces, rather than by presiding over their individual empires. It was traditionally the job of top executives or specialists to scan the business environment for new ideas, opportunities, and resources. This kind of environmental scanning is now an important part of a manager's job at every level and in every function. And the environment to be scanned includes various company divisions, many potential outside partners, and large parts of the world. At the same time, people are encouraged to think about what they know that might have value elsewhere. An engineer designing windshield wipers, for example, might discover properties of rubber adhesion to glass that could be useful in other manufacturing areas.

Every manager must think cross-functionally because every department has to play a strategic role, understanding and contributing to other facets of the business. In Hank's company, the technical managers and staff working on design engineering used to concentrate only on their own areas of expertise. Under the new system, they have to keep in mind what manufacturing does and how it does it. They need to visit plants and build relationships so they can ask informed questions.

One multinational corporation, eager to extend the uses of its core product, put its R&D staff and laboratory personnel in direct contact with marketing experts to discuss lines of research. Similarly, the superior economic track record of Raytheon's New Products Center—dozens of new products and patents yielding profits many times their development costs—derives from the connections it builds between its inventors and the engineering and marketing staffs of the business units it serves.

This strategic and collaborative role is particularly important for the managers and professionals on corporate staffs. They need to serve as integrators and facilitators, not as watchdogs and interventionists. They need to sell their services, justify themselves to the business units they serve, literally compete with outside suppliers. General Foods recently put overhead charges for corporate staff services on a pay-as-you-use basis. Formerly, these charges were either assigned uniformly to users and nonusers alike, or the services were mandatory. Product managers sometimes had to work through as many as eight layers of management and corporate staff to get business

> **To add value, managers think and work across boundaries.**

plans approved. Now these staffs must prove to the satisfaction of their internal customers that their services add value.

By contrast, some banks still have corporate training departments that do very little except get in the way. They do no actual training, for example, yet they still exercise veto power over urgent divisional training decisions and consultant contracts.

As managers and professionals spend more time working across boundaries with peers and partners over whom they have no direct control, their negotiating skills become essential assets. Alliances and partnerships transform impersonal, arm's-length contracts into relationships involving joint planning and joint decision making. Internal competitors and adversaries become allies on whom managers depend for their own success. At the same time, more managers at more levels are active in the kind of external diplomacy that only the CEO or selected staffs used to conduct.

In the collaborative forums that result, managers are more personally exposed. It is trust that makes partnerships work. Since collaborative ventures often bring together groups with different methods, cultures, symbols, even languages, good deal making depends on empathy—the ability to step into other people's shoes and appreciate their goals. This applies not only to intricate global joint ventures but also to the efforts of engineering and manufacturing to work together more effectively. Effective communication in a cooperative effort rests on more than a simple exchange of information; people must be adept at anticipating the responses of other groups. "Before I get too excited about our department's design ideas," an engineering manager told me, "I'm learning to ask myself, 'What's the marketing position on this? What

> **Today's executive must bargain, negotiate, and sell ideas like any other politician.**

will manufacturing say?' That sometimes forces me to make changes before I even talk to them."

An increase in the number of channels for strategic contact within the postentrepreneurial organization means more opportunities for people with ideas or information to trigger action: salespeople encouraging account managers to build strategic partnerships with customers, for example, or technicians searching for ways to tap new-venture funds to develop software. Moreover, top executives who have to spend more time on cross-boundary relationships are forced to delegate more responsibility to lower level managers. Delegation is one more blow to hierarchy, of course, since subordinates with greater responsibility are bolder about speaking up, challenging authority, and charting their own course.

For example, it is common for new-venture teams to complain publicly about corporate support departments and to reject their use in favor of external service providers, often to the consternation of more orthodox superiors. A more startling example occured in a health care company where members of a task force charged with finding synergies among three lines of business shocked corporate executives by criticizing upper management behavior in their report. Service on the task force had created collective awareness of a shared problem and had given people the courage to confront it.

The search for internal synergies, the development of strategic alliances, and the push for new ventures all emphasize the political side of a leader's work. Executives must be able to juggle a set of constituencies rather than control a set of subordinates. They have to bargain, negotiate, and sell instead of making unilateral decisions and issuing commands. The leader's task, as Chester Barnard recognized long ago, is to develop a network of cooperative relationships among all the people, groups, and organizations that have something to contribute to an economic enterprise. Postentrepreneurial strategies magnify the complexity of this task. After leading Teknowledge, a producer of expert systems software, through development alliances with six corporations including General Motors and Procter & Gamble, company chairman Lee Hecht said he felt like the mayor of a small city. "I have a constituency that won't quit. It takes a hell of a lot of balancing." The kind of power achieved through a network of stakeholders is very different from the kind of power managers wield in a traditional bureaucracy. The new way gets more done, but it also takes more time. And it creates an illusion about freedom and security.

The absence of day-to-day constraints, the admonition to assume responsibility, the pretense of equality, the elimination of visible status markers, the prevalence of candid dialogues across hierarchical levels—these can give employees a false sense that all hierarchy is a thing of the past. Yet at the same time, employees still count on hierarchy to shield them when things go wrong. This combination would create the perfect marriage of freedom and support—freedom when people want to take risks, support when the risks don't work out.

In reality, less benevolent combinations are also possible, combinations not of freedom and support but of insecurity and loss of control. There is often a pretense in postentrepreneurial companies that sta-

> **The promise of freedom has a dark side: insecurity and loss of control.**

tus differences have nothing to do with power, that the deference paid to top executives derives from their superior qualifications rather than from the power they have over the fates of others. But the people at the top of the organization chart still wield power—and sometimes in ways that managers below them experience as arbitrary. Unprecedented individual freedom also applies to top managers, who are now free to make previously unimaginable deals, order unimaginable cuts, or launch unimaginable takeovers. The reorganizations that companies undertake in their search for new synergies can uncover the potential unpredictability and capriciousness of corporate careers. A man whose company was undergoing drastic restructuring told me, "For all of my ownership share and strategic centrality and voice in decisions, I can still be faced with a shift in direction not of my own making. I can still be reorganized into a corner. I can still be relocated into oblivion. I can still be reviewed out of my special project budget."

These realities of power, change, and job security are important because they affect the way people view their leaders. When the illusion of simultaneous freedom and protection fades, the result can be a loss of motivation.

Sources of Motivation

One of the essential, unchanging tasks of leaders is to motivate and guide performance. But motivational tools are changing fast. More and more businesses are doing away with the old bureaucratic incentives and using entrepreneurial opportunity to attract the best talent. Managers must exercise more leadership even as they watch their bureaucratic power slip away. Leadership, in short, is more difficult yet more critical than ever.

Because of the unpredictability of even the most benign restructuring, managers are less able to guarantee a particular job—or any job at all—no matter what a subordinate's performance level. The reduction in hierarchical levels curtails a manager's ability to promise promotion. New compensation systems that make bonuses and raises dependent on objective performance measures and on team appraisals deprive managers of their role as the sole arbiter of higher pay. Cross-functional and cross-company teams can rob managers of their right to direct or even understand the work their so-called subordinates do. In any case, the shift from routine work, which was amenable to oversight, to "knowledge" work, which often is not, erodes a manager's claim to superior expertise. And partnerships and ventures that put lower level people in direct contact with each other across departmental and company boundaries cut heavily into the managerial monopoly on information. At a consumer packaged-goods manufacturer that replaced several levels of hierarchy with teams, plant team members in direct contact with the sales force often had data on product ordering trends before the higher level brand managers who set product policy.

As if the loss of carrots and sticks was not enough, many managers can no longer even give their people clear job standards and easily mastered procedural rules. Postentrepreneurial corporations seek problem-solving, initiative-taking employees who will go the unexpected extra mile for the customer. To complicate the situation further still, the complexities of work in the new organization—projects and relationships clamoring for attention in every direction—exacerbate the feeling of overload.

With the old motivational tool kit depleted, leaders need new and more effective incentives to encourage high performance and build commitment. There are five new tools:

Mission. Helping people believe in the importance of their work is essential, especially when other forms of certainty and security have disappeared. Good leaders can inspire others with the power and excitement of their vision and give people a sense of purpose and pride in their work. Pride is often a better source of motivation than the traditional corporate career ladder and the promotion-based reward system. Technical professionals, for example, are often motivated most effectively by the desire to see their work contribute to an excellent final product.

Agenda Control. As career paths lose their certainty and companies' futures grow less predictable, people can at least be in charge of their own professional lives. More and more professionals are passing up jobs with glamour and prestige in favor of jobs that give them greater control over their own activities and direction. Leaders give their subordinates this opportunity when they give them release time to work on pet projects, when they emphasize results instead of procedures, and when they delegate work and the decisions about how to do it. Choice of their next project is a potent reward for people who perform well.

Share of Value Creation. Entrepreneurial incentives that give teams a piece of the action are highly appropriate in collaborative companies. Because extra rewards are based only on measurable results, this approach also conserves resources. Innovative companies are experimenting with incentives like phantom stock for development of new ventures and other strategic achievements, equity participation in project returns, and bonuses pegged to key performance targets. Given the cross-functional nature of many projects today, rewards of this kind must sometimes be systemwide, but individual managers can also ask for a bonus pool for their own areas, contingent, of course, on meeting performance goals. And everyone can share the kinds of rewards that are abundant and free—awards and recognition.

Learning. The chance to learn new skills or apply them in new arenas is an important motivator in a turbulent environment because it's oriented toward securing the future. "The learning organization" promises to become a 1990s business buzzword as companies seek to learn more systematically from their experience and to encourage continuous learning for their people. In the world of high technology, where people understand uncertainty, the attractiveness of any company often lies in its capacity to provide learning and experience. By this calculus, access to training, mentors, and challenging projects is more important than pay or benefits. Some prominent companies—General Electric, for example—have always been able to attract top talent, even when they could not promise upward mobility, because people see them as a training ground, a good place to learn, and a valuable addition to a résumé.

Reputation. Reputation is a key resource in professional careers, and the chance to enhance it can be an outstanding motivator. The professional's reliance on reputation stands in marked contrast to the bureaucrat's anonymity. Professionals have to make a name for themselves, while traditional corporate managers and employees stayed behind the scenes. Indeed, the accumulation of reputational "capital" provides not only an immediate ego boost but also the kind of publicity that can bring other rewards, even other job offers. Managers can enhance reputation—and improve motivation—by creating stars, by providing abundant public recognition and visible awards, by crediting the authors of innovation, by publicizing people outside their own departments, and by plugging people into organizational and professional networks.

The new, collaborative organization is predicated on a logic of flexible work assignments, not of fixed job responsibilities. To promote innovation and responsiveness, two of today's competitive imperatives, managers need to see this new organization as a

> **When an engineer saw a TV ad for his design, he shouted to his family, "Hey! That's mine!"** *That's* **compensation.**

cluster of activity sets, not as a rigid structure. The work of leadership in this new corporation will be to organize both sequential and synchronous projects of varying length and breadth, through which varying combinations of people will move, depending on the tasks, challenges, and opportunities facing the area and its partners at any given moment.

Leaders need to carve out projects with tangible accomplishments, milestones, and completion dates and then delegate responsibility for these projects to the people who flesh them out. Clearly delimited projects can counter overload by focusing effort and can provide short-term motivation when the fate of the long-term mission is uncertain. Project responsibility leads to ownership of the results and sometimes substitutes for other forms of reward. In companies where product development teams define and run their own projects, members commonly say that the greatest compensation they get is seeing the advertisements for their products. "Hey, that's mine! I did that!" one engineer told me he trumpeted to his family the first time he saw a commercial for his group's innovation.

This sense of ownership, along with a definite time frame, can spur higher levels of effort. Whenever people are engaged in creative or problem-solving projects that will have tangible results by deadline dates, they tend to come in at all hours, to think about the project in their spare time, to invest in it vast sums of physical and emotional energy. Knowing that the project will end and that completion will be an occasion for reward and recognition makes it possible to work much harder.

Leaders in the new organization do not lack motivational tools, but the tools are different from those of traditional corporate bureaucrats. The new rewards are based not on status but on contribution, and they consist not of regular promotion and automatic pay raises but of excitement about mission and a share of the glory and the gains of success. The new security is not employment security (a guaranteed job no matter what) but *employability* security—increased value in the internal and external labor markets. Commitment to the organization still matters, but today managers build commitment by offering project opportunities. The new loyalty is not to the boss or to the company but to projects that actualize a mission and offer challenge, growth, and credit for results.

The old bases of managerial authority are eroding, and new tools of leadership are taking their place. Managers whose power derived from hierarchy and who were accustomed to a limited area of personal control are learning to shift their perspectives and widen their horizons. The new managerial work consists of looking outside a defined area of responsibility to sense opportunities and of forming project teams drawn from any relevant sphere to address them. It involves communication and collaboration across functions, across divisions, and across companies whose activities and resources overlap. Thus rank, title, or official charter will be less important factors in success at the new managerial work than having the knowledge, skills, and sensitivity to mobilize people and motivate them to do their best.

Reprint 89606

Entrepreneurship reconsidered: the team as hero

Robert B. Reich

" 'Wake up there, youngster,' said a rough voice.

"Ragged Dick opened his eyes slowly and stared stupidly in the face of the speaker, but did not offer to get up.

" 'Wake up, you young vagabond!' said the man a little impatiently; 'I suppose you'd lay there all day, if I hadn't called you.' "

So begins the story of *Ragged Dick, or Street Life in New York,* Horatio Alger's first book – the first of 135 tales written in the late 1800s that together sold close to 20 million copies. Like all the books that followed, *Ragged Dick* told the story of a young man who, by pluck and luck, rises from his lowly station to earn a respectable job and the promise of a better life.

Nearly a century later, another bestselling American business story offered a different concept of heroism and a different description of the route to success. This story begins:

"All the way to the horizon in the last light, the sea was just degrees of gray, rolling and frothy on the surface. From the cockpit of a small white sloop – she was 35 feet long – the waves looked like hills coming up from behind, and most of the crew preferred not to glance at them....Running under shortened sails in front of the northeaster, the boat rocked one way, gave a thump, and then it rolled the other. The pots and pans in the galley clanged. A six-pack of beer, which someone had forgotten to stow away, slid back and forth across the cabin floor, over and over again. Sometime late that night, one of the crew raised a voice against the wind and asked, 'What are we trying to prove?' "

The book is Tracy Kidder's *The Soul of a New Machine,* a 1981 tale of how a team – a crew – of hardworking inventors built a computer by pooling their efforts. The opening scene is a metaphor for the team's treacherous journey.

Separated by 100 years, totally different in their explanations of what propels the American economy, these two stories symbolize the choice that Americans will face in the 1990s; each celebrates a fundamentally different version of American entrepreneurship. Which version we choose to embrace will help determine how quickly and how well the United States adapts to the challenge of global competition.

Which will we celebrate: individual heroes or teams?

Horatio Alger's notion of success is the traditional one: the familiar tale of triumphant individuals, of enterprising heroes who win riches and rewards through a combination of Dale Carnegie-esque self-improvement, Norman Vincent Peale-esque faith, Sylvester Stallone-esque assertiveness, and plain, old-fashioned good luck. Tracy Kidder's story, by contrast, teaches that economic success comes through the talent, energy, and commitment of a team – through *collective* entrepreneurship.

Stories like these do more than merely entertain or divert us. Like ancient myths that captured and contained an essential truth, they shape how we see and understand our lives, how we make sense of our experience. Stories can mobilize us to action and affect our behavior – more powerfully than simple and straightforward information ever can.

Robert B. Reich teaches political economy and management at the John F. Kennedy School of Government, Harvard University. His most recent book is Tales of a New America *(Times Books, 1987), which explores in greater depth the issues discussed in this article.*

To the extent that we continue to celebrate the traditional myth of the entrepreneurial hero, we will slow the progress of change and adaptation that is essential to our economic success. If we are to compete effectively in today's world, we must begin to celebrate collective entrepreneurship, endeavors in which the whole of the effort is greater than the sum of individual contributions. We need to honor our teams more, our aggressive leaders and maverick geniuses less.

Heroes & drones

The older and still dominant American myth involves two kinds of actors: entrepreneurial heroes and industrial drones—the inspired and the perspired.

In this myth, entrepreneurial heroes personify freedom and creativity. They come up with the Big Ideas and build the organizations—the Big Machines—that turn them into reality. They take the initiative, come up with technological and organizational innovations, devise new solutions to old problems. They are the men and women who start vibrant new companies, turn around failing companies, and shake up staid ones. To all endeavors they apply daring and imagination.

The myth of the entrepreneurial hero is as old as America and has served us well in a number of ways. We like to see ourselves as born mavericks and fixers. Our entrepreneurial drive has long been our distinguishing trait. Generations of inventors and investors have kept us on the technological frontier. In a world of naysayers and traditionalists, the American character has always stood out—cheerfully optimistic, willing to run risks, ready to try anything. During World War II, it was the rough-and-ready American GI who could fix the stalled jeep in Normandy while the French regiment only looked on.

Horatio Alger captured this spirit in hundreds of stories. With titles like *Bound to Rise*, *Luck and Pluck*, and *Sink or Swim*, they inspired millions of readers with a gloriously simple message: in America you can go from rags to riches. The plots were essentially the same; like any successful entrepreneur, Alger knew when he was onto a good thing. A fatherless, penniless boy—possessed of great determination, faith, and courage—seeks his fortune. All manner of villain tries to tempt him, divert him, or separate him from his small savings. But in the end, our hero prevails—not just through pluck; luck plays a part too—and by the end of the story he is launched on his way to fame and fortune.

At the turn of the century, Americans saw fiction and reality sometimes converging. Edward Harriman began as a $5-a-week office boy and came to head a mighty railroad empire. John D. Rockefeller rose from a clerk in a commission merchant's house to become one of the world's richest men. Andrew Carnegie started as a $1.20-a-week bobbin boy in a Pittsburgh cotton mill and became the nation's foremost steel magnate. In the early 1900s, when boys were still reading the Alger tales, Henry Ford made his fortune mass-producing the Model T, and in the process became both a national folk hero and a potential presidential candidate.

Alger's stories gave the country a noble ideal—a society in which imagination and effort summoned their just reward. The key virtue was self-reliance; the admirable man was the self-made man; the goal was to be your own boss. Andrew Carnegie articulated the prevailing view:

"Is any would-be businessman...content in forecasting his future, to figure himself as labouring all his life for a fixed salary? Not one, I am sure. In this you have the dividing line between business and non-business; the one is master and depends on profits, the other is servant and depends on salary."[1]

The entrepreneurial hero still captures the American imagination. Inspired by the words of his immigrant father, who told him, "You could be anything you want to be, if you wanted it bad enough and were willing to work for it," Lido Iacocca worked his way up to the presidency of Ford Motor Company, from which he was abruptly fired by Henry Ford II, only to go on to rescue Chrysler from bankruptcy, thumb his nose at Ford in a best-selling autobiography, renovate the Statue of Liberty, and gain mention as a possible presidential candidate.[2] Could Horatio Alger's heroes have done any better?

Peter Ueberroth, son of a traveling aluminum salesman, worked his way through college, single-handedly built a $300 million business, went on to organize the 1984 Olympics, became *Time* magazine's Man of the Year and the commissioner of baseball. Steven Jobs built his own computer company from scratch and became a multimillionaire before his thirtieth birthday. Stories of entrepreneurial heroism come from across the economy and across the country: professors who create whole new industries and become instant millionaires when their inventions go from the laboratory to the marketplace; youthful engi-

---

1 Andrew Carnegie, *The Business of Empire* (New York: Doubleday, Page, 1902), p. 192.

2 See Lee Iacocca and William Novak, *Iacocca: An Autobiography* (New York: Bantam Books, 1984).

3 George Gilder, *The Spirit of Enterprise* (New York: Simon and Schuster, 1984), p. 213.

4 Ibid., p. 147.

neers who quit their jobs, strike out on their own, and strike it rich.

In the American economic mythology, these heroes occupy center stage: "Fighters, fanatics, men with a lust for contest, a gleam of creation, and a drive to justify their break from the mother company."[3] Prosperity for all depends on the entrepreneurial vision of a few rugged individuals.

If the entrepreneurial heroes hold center stage in this drama, the rest of the vast work force plays a supporting role – supporting and unheralded. Average workers in this myth are drones – cogs in the Big Machines, so many interchangeable parts, unable to perform without direction from above. They are put to work for their hands, not for their minds or imaginations. Their jobs typically appear by the dozens in the help-wanted sections of daily newspapers. Their routines are unvaried. They have little opportunity to use judgment or creativity. To the entrepreneurial hero belongs all the inspiration; the drones are governed by the rules and valued for their reliability and pliability.

Our Big Ideas travel quickly to foreign competitors.

These average workers are no villains – but they are certainly no heroes. Uninteresting and uninterested, goes the myth, they lack creative spark and entrepreneurial vision. These are, for example, the nameless and faceless workers who lined up for work in response to Henry Ford's visionary offer of a $5-per-day paycheck. At best, they put in a decent effort in executing the entrepreneurial hero's grand design. At worst, they demand more wages and benefits for less work, do the minimum expected of them, or function as bland bureaucrats mired in standard operating procedures.

The entrepreneurial hero and the worker drone together personify the mythic version of how the American economic system works. The system needs both types. But rewards and treatment for the two are as different as the roles themselves: the entrepreneurs should be rewarded with fame and fortune; drones should be disciplined through clear rules and punishments. Considering the overwhelming importance attached to the entrepreneur in this paradigm, the difference seems appropriate. For, as George Gilder has written, "All of us are dependent for our livelihood and progress not on a vast and predictable machine, but on the creativity and courage of the particular men who accept the risks which generate our riches."[4]

Why Horatio Alger can't help us anymore

There is just one fatal problem with this dominant myth: it is obsolete. The economy that it describes no longer exists. By clinging to the myth, we subscribe to an outmoded view of how to win economic success – a view that, on a number of counts, endangers our economic future:

☐ In today's global economy, the Big Ideas pioneered by American entrepreneurs travel quickly to foreign lands. In the hands of global competitors, these ideas can undergo continuous adaptation and improvement and reemerge as new Big Ideas or as a series of incrementally improved small ideas.

☐ The machines that American entrepreneurs have always set up so efficiently to execute their Big Ideas are equally footloose. Process technology moves around the globe to find the cheapest labor and the friendliest markets. As ideas migrate overseas, the economic and technological resources needed to implement the ideas migrate too.

☐ Workers in other parts of the world are apt to be cheaper or more productive – or both – than workers in the United States. Around the globe, millions of potential workers are ready to underbid American labor.

☐ Some competitor nations – Japan, in particular – have created relationships among engineers, managers, production workers, and marketing and sales people that do away with the old distinction between entrepreneurs and drones. The dynamic result is yet another basis for challenging American assumptions about what leads to competitive success.

Because of these global changes, the United States is now susceptible to competitive challenge on two grounds. First, by borrowing the Big Ideas and process technology that come from the United States and providing the hardworking, low-paid workers, developing nations can achieve competitive advantage. Second, by embracing collective entrepreneurship, the Japanese especially have found a different way to achieve competitive advantage while maintaining high real wages.

Americans continue to lead the world in breakthroughs and cutting-edge scientific discoveries. But the Big Ideas that start in this country now quickly travel abroad, where they not only get produced at high speed, at low cost, and with great efficiency, but also undergo continuous development and improvement. And all too often, American companies get bogged down somewhere between invention and production.

42 Participative management

Several product histories make the point. Americans invented the solid-state transistor in 1947. Then in 1953, Western Electric licensed the technology to Sony for $25,000 – and the rest is history. A few years later, RCA licensed several Japanese companies to make color televisions – and that was the beginning of the end of color television production in the United States. Routine assembly of color televisions eventually shifted to Taiwan and Mexico. At the same time, Sony and other Japanese companies pushed the technology in new directions, continuously refining it into a stream of consumer products.

In 1968, Unimation licensed Kawasaki Heavy Industries to make industrial robots. The Japanese took the initial technology and kept moving it forward. The pattern has been the same for one Big Idea after another. Americans came up with the Big Ideas for videocassette recorders, basic oxygen furnaces, and continuous casters for making steel, microwave ovens, automobile stamping machines, computerized machine tools, integrated circuits. But these Big Ideas – and many, many others – quickly found their way into production in foreign countries: routine, standardized production in developing nations or continuous refinement and complex applications in Japan. Either way, the United States has lost ground.

Older industrial economies, like our own, have two options: they can try to match the low wages and discipline under which workers elsewhere in the world are willing to labor, or they can compete on the basis of how quickly and how well they transform ideas into incrementally better products. The second option is, in fact, the only one that offers the possibility of high real incomes in America. But here's the catch: a handful of lone entrepreneurs producing a few industry-making Big Ideas can't execute this second option. Innovation must become both continuous and collective. And that requires embracing a new ideal: collective entrepreneurship.

The new economic paradigm

If America is to win in the new global competition, we need to begin telling one another a new story in which companies compete by drawing on the talent and creativity of all their employees, not just a few maverick inventors and dynamic CEOs. Competitive advantage today comes from continuous, incremental innovation and refinement of a variety of ideas that spread throughout the organization. The entrepreneurial organization is both experience-based and decentralized, so that every advance builds on every pre-

"We've decided to tell individuals we treat them like institutions, and tell institutions we treat them like individuals."

vious advance, and everyone in the company has the opportunity and capacity to participate.

While this story represents a departure from tradition, it already exists, in fact, to a greater or lesser extent in every well-run American and Japanese corporation. The difference is that we don't recognize and celebrate this story – and the Japanese do.

Consider just a few of the evolutionary paths that collective entrepreneurship can take: vacuum-tube radios become transistorized radios, then stereo pocket radios audible through earphones, then compact discs and compact disc players, and then optical-disc computer memories. Color televisions evolve into digital televisions capable of showing several pictures simultaneously; videocassette recorders into camcorders. A single strand of technological evolution connects electronic sewing machines, electronic typewriters, and flexible electronic workstations. Basic steels give way to high-strength and corrosion-resistant steels, then to new materials composed of steel mixed with silicon and custom-made polymers. Basic chemicals evolve into high-performance ceramics, to single-crystal silicon and high-grade crystal glass. Copper wire gives way to copper cables, then to fiber-optic cables.

These patterns reveal no clear life cycles with beginnings, middles, and ends. Unlike Big Ideas that beget standardized commodities, these products undergo a continuous process of incremental change and adaptation. Workers at all levels add value not solely or even mostly by tending machines and carrying out routines, but by continuously discovering opportunities for improvement in product and process.

In this context, it makes no sense to speak of an "industry" like steel or automobiles or televisions or even banking. There are no clear borders around any of these clusters of goods or services. When products and processes are so protean, companies grow or decline not with the market for some specific good, but with the creative and adaptive capacity of their workers.

Workers in such organizations constantly reinvent the company; one idea leads to another. Producing the latest generation of automobiles involves making electronic circuits that govern fuel consumption and monitor engine performance; developments in these devices lead to improved sensing equipment and software for monitoring heartbeats and moisture in the air. Producing cars also involves making flexible robots for assembling parts and linking them by computer; steady improvements in these technologies, in turn, lead to expert production systems that can be applied anywhere. What is considered the "automobile industry" thus becomes a wide variety of technologies evolving toward all sorts of applications that flow from the same strand of technological development toward different markets.

In this paradigm, entrepreneurship isn't the sole province of the company's founder or its top managers. Rather, it is a capability and attitude that is diffused throughout the company. Experimentation and development go on all the time as the company searches for new ways to capture and build on the knowledge already accumulated by its workers.

Distinctions between innovation and production, between top managers and production workers blur. Because production is a continuous process of reinvention, entrepreneurial efforts are focused on many thousands of small ideas rather than on just a few big ones. And because valuable information and expertise are dispersed throughout the organization, top management does not solve problems; it creates an environment in which people can identify and solve problems themselves.

Most of the training for working in this fashion takes place on the job. Formal education may prepare people to absorb and integrate experience, but it does not supply the experience. No one can anticipate the precise skills that workers will need to succeed on the job when information processing, know-how, and creativity are the value added. Any job that could be fully prepared for in advance is, by definition, a job that could be exported to a low-wage country or programmed into robots and computers; a routine job is a job destined to disappear.

In collective entrepreneurship, individual skills are integrated into a group; this collective capacity to innovate becomes something greater than the sum of its parts. Over time, as group members work through various problems and approaches, they learn about each others' abilities. They learn how they can help one another perform better, what each can contribute to a particular project, how they can best take advantage of one another's experience. Each participant is constantly on the lookout for small adjustments that will speed and smooth the evolution of the whole. The net result of many such small-scale adaptations, effected throughout the organization, is to propel the enterprise forward.

You have to constantly reinvent the company.

Collective entrepreneurship thus entails close working relationships among people at all stages of the process. If customers' needs are to be recognized and met, designers and engineers must be familiar with sales and marketing. Salespeople must also have a complete understanding of the enterprise's capacity to design and deliver specialized products. The company's ability to adapt to new opportunities and capitalize on them depends on its capacity to share information and involve everyone in the organization in a systemwide search for ways to improve, adjust, adapt, and upgrade.

Collective entrepreneurship also entails a different organizational structure. Under the old paradigm, companies are organized into a series of hierarchical tiers so that supervisors at each level can make sure that subordinates act according to plan. It is a structure designed to control. But enterprises designed for continuous innovation and incremental improvement use a structure designed to spur innovation at all levels. Gaining insight into improvement of products and processes is more important than rigidly following rules. Coordination and communication replace command and control. Consequently, there are few middle-level managers and only modest differences in the status and income of senior managers and junior employees.

Simple accounting systems are no longer adequate or appropriate for monitoring and evaluating job performance: tasks are intertwined and interdependent, and the quality of work is often more important than the quantity of work. In a system where each worker depends on many others—and where the success of the company depends on all—the only appropriate measurement of accomplishment is a collective one. At the same time, the reward system reflects this new approach: profit sharing, gain sharing, and performance bonuses all demonstrate that the success of the company comes from the broadest contribution of all the company's employees, not just those at the top.

Finally, under collective entrepreneurship, workers do not fear technology and automation as a threat to their jobs. When workers add value through judgment and knowledge, computers become tools that expand their discretion. Computer-generated information can give workers rich feedback about their own efforts, how they affect others in the production process, and how the entire process can be improved. One of the key lessons to come out of the General Motors-Toyota joint venture in California is that the Japanese automaker does not rely on automation and technology to replace workers in the plant. In fact, human workers still occupy the most critical jobs – those where judgment and evaluation are essential. Instead, Toyota uses technology to allow workers to focus on those important tasks where choices have to be made. Under this approach, technology gives workers the chance to use their imagination and their insight on behalf of the company.

The team as hero

In 1986, one of America's largest and oldest enterprises announced that it was changing the way it assigned its personnel: the U.S. Army discarded a system that assigned soldiers to their units individually in favor of a system that keeps teams of soldiers together for their entire tours of duty. An Army spokesperson explained, "We discovered that individuals perform better when they are part of a stable group. They are more reliable. They also take responsibility for the success of the overall operation."

In one of its recent advertisements, BellSouth captures the new story. "BellSouth is not a bunch of individuals out for themselves," the ad proclaimed. "We're a team."

Collective entrepreneurship is already here. It shows up in the way our best run companies now organize their work, regard their workers, design their enterprises. Yet the old myth of the entrepreneurial hero remains powerful. Many Americans would prefer to think that Lee Iacocca single-handedly saved Chrysler from bankruptcy than to accept the real story: a large team of people with diverse backgrounds and interests joined together to rescue the ailing company.

Bookstores bulge with new volumes paying homage to American CEOs. It is a familiar story; it is an engaging story. And no doubt, when seen through the eyes of the CEO, it accurately portrays how that individual experienced the company's success. But what gets left out time after time are the experiences of the rest of the team – the men and women at every level of the company whose contributions to the company created the success that the CEO so eagerly claims. Where are the books that celebrate their stories?

Most people would rather think that Lee Iacocca saved Chrysler than know the truth.

You can also find inspirational management texts designed to tell top executives how to be kinder to employees, treat them with respect, listen to them, and make them feel appreciated. By reading these books, executives can learn how to search for excellence, create excellence, achieve excellence, or become impassioned about excellence – preferably within one minute. Managers are supposed to walk around, touch employees, get directly involved, effervesce with praise and encouragement, stage celebrations, and indulge in hoopla.

Some of this is sound; some of it is hogwash. But most of it, even the best, is superficial. Lacking any real context, unattached to any larger understanding of why relationships between managers and workers matter, the prescriptions often remain shallow and are treated as such. The effervescent executive is likely to be gone in a few years, many of the employees will be gone, and the owners may be different as well. Too often the company is assumed to be a collection of assets, available to the highest bidder. When times require it, employees will be sacked. Everybody responds accordingly. Underneath the veneer of participatory management, it is business as usual – and business as usual represents a threat to America's long-term capacity to compete.

If the United States is to compete effectively in the world in a way designed to enhance the real incomes of Americans, we must bring collective entrepreneurship to the forefront of the economy. That will require us to change our attitudes, to downplay the myth of the entrepreneurial hero, and to celebrate our creative teams.

First, we will need to look for and promote new kinds of stories. In modern-day America, stories of collective entrepreneurship typically appear in the sports pages of the daily newspaper; time after time, in accounts of winning efforts we learn that the team with the best blend of talent won – the team that emphasized teamwork—not the team with the best individual athlete. The cultural challenge is to move these stories from the sports page to the business page. We need to shift the limelight from maverick founders and shake-'em-up CEOs to groups of engineers, production workers, and marketers who successfully innovate new products and services. We need to look for opportunities to tell stories about American business from the perspective of all the workers who make up the team, rather than solely from the perspective of top managers. The stories are there—we need only change our focus, alter our frame of reference, in order to find them.

Second, we will need to understand that the most powerful stories get told, not in books and newspapers, but in the everyday world of work. Whether managers know it or not, every decision they make suggests a story to the rest of the enterprise. Decisions to award generous executive bonuses or to provide plush executive dining rooms and executive parking places tell the old story of entrepreneurial heroism. A decision to lay off 10% of the work force tells the old story of the drone worker. Several years ago, when General Motors reached agreement on a contract with the United Auto Workers that called for a new relationship based on cooperation and shared sacrifice, and then, on the same day, announced a new formula for generous executive bonuses, long-time union members simply nodded to themselves. The actions told the whole story. It is not enough to acknowledge the importance of collective entrepreneurship; clear and consistent signals must reinforce the new story.

Collective entrepreneurship represents the path toward an economic future that is promising for both managers and workers. For managers, this path means continually retraining employees for more complex tasks; automating in ways that cut routine tasks and enhance worker flexibility and creativity; diffusing responsibility for innovation; taking seriously labor's concern for job security; and giving workers a stake in improved productivity through profit-linked bonuses and stock plans.

For workers, this path means accepting flexible job classifications and work rules; agreeing to wage rates linked to profits and productivity improvements; and generally taking greater responsibility for the soundness and efficiency of the enterprise. This path also involves a closer and more permanent relationship with other parties that have a stake in the company's performance—suppliers, dealers, creditors, even the towns and cities in which the company resides.

Under collective entrepreneurship, all those associated with the company become partners in its future. The distinction between entrepreneurs and drones breaks down. Each member of the enterprise participates in its evolution. All have a commitment to the company's continued success. It is the one approach that can maintain and improve America's competitive performance—and America's standard of living—over the long haul.

Reprint 87309

Richard J. Boyle

Wrestling with jellyfish

An executive finds that becoming a participative manager is a slippery business

We have heard a lot recently about quality circles, quality of work life programs, job redesign, and other efforts to improve working conditions and productivity in our nation's businesses. In this article we hear the personal testimony of one participant in a change effort of a different sort, the transformation of the management style of a large corporation.

When the author joined Honeywell, Inc. more than two decades ago, "steely, no-nonsense executives" ran the company in an autocratic manner. This article chronicles the attempts of employees in one division to relax the company's traditional militaristic style of management and substitute a more participative approach. Like many revolutions, however, this one was fraught with unanticipated problems and issues. The absence of clear guidelines, policies, and support structures made becoming a participative manager, in the words of one employee, like wrestling with jellyfish. As the author recounts,

Illustrations by Katherine Mahoney.

Honeywell managers and employees encountered many frustrations and explored several blind alleys before discovering some central truths: that means are as important as ends and that participative management must be managed.

Mr. Boyle is vice president and group executive, Honeywell Defense and Marine Systems Group, Honeywell, Inc. in Minneapolis. At Honeywell since 1957, he served in a variety of engineering and operations management positions, including vice president and general manager of the Defense Electronic Division and the Defense Systems Division, before assuming his present job in 1983. Mr. Boyle is a member of the Institute of Electronic and Electrical Engineers and of two honorary engineering societies, Tau Beta Pi and Eta Kappa Nu, and he is a director of several corporations.

Author's note: I would like to recognize the many valuable contributions of Rosabeth Kanter of Yale University and of Goodmeasure, Inc. particularly for her insights into the new demands of management in the 1980s. I would also like to thank Charlie Quimby of Honeywell and Tana Pesso of Goodmeasure who were very helpful in making the article so readable.

Many organizations today want to break out of the beat-'em-up school of management and move toward a more participative management style. But like abused children who grow up to become abusive parents, managers raised in a less enlightened manner may have difficulty operating under a new set of rules.

At Honeywell, we have been working to change from what I call the Patton style of management to a more collaborative way of operating. We are still in the midst of this process. The way we manage people is still less than perfect. But now our employees can have a real share of the action rather than feeling blocked or frustrated by a rigid bureaucracy. And the results, both in quantifiable terms of productivity improvement and in less measurable terms of work climate and quality of innovation, have been extremely positive.

I'd like to share my observations about the changing of Honeywell's management style, the difficulties we encountered along the way, and the solutions we employed to bring us where we are today. Understanding our mistakes is crucial to understanding our story, because some of the mistakes were an integral part of our evolution. In other words, making participation an organic way of working had to come about through an organic process—at least in our organization. Taking a cookbook approach or bringing in executive quick-change artists would not have achieved the same results. On the other hand, I don't believe others must repeat our mistakes to share our central discovery—that the participative process must be managed.

We made this discovery between 1980 and 1982 in a division of Honeywell now called the Defense and Marine Systems Group (then the Defense Systems Division). That division has since expanded and reorganized as a group of divisions, in part because of the success it has achieved in the past several years.

The group has about 8,000 employees concentrated in Minnesota, California, and Washington. It represents roughly 10% of Honeywell's people and 12% of Honeywell's $6 billion in revenues. About half of the group's population is in the Minneapolis area, where Honeywell has its corporate headquarters and several other large operations.

The group's defense business includes making torpedoes, ammunition, and other weapons for the U.S. military as well as designing computer-based training systems. Our commercial business is aimed at the offshore oil and maritime industries, for which we provide services and produce drilling vessel stabilization systems and undersea robots and television cameras. We also offer engineering services, primarily in water resource management. Our work force is a highly educated, highly motivated group of people. About one in five is an engineer. The group's 1,600 factory employees in Minneapolis are unionized. It is common to find employees with 20 years' tenure in the older divisions.

Patton-style management

When I began my career at Honeywell in the late 1950s and as I advanced to more senior positions, steely, no-nonsense executives were the norm. Many examples of their autocratic management are permanently blazed in corporate legend. One "productivity initiative" from those days (long since reversed) was the removal of bathroom stall doors to discourage reading on company time. Today's middle and upper managers were trained during that period, and getting them to commit themselves to a new management style was no simple matter. After all, why should they trade their pearl-handled revolvers for a copy of *The One Minute Manager* when a swift, Patton-like kick took only a few seconds?

Employees had seen many management improvement programs come and go. Honeywell's paternalistic organization had taken care of its employees, who were only sporadically encouraged to demonstrate initiative. And when they did so, urged on by some program or other, they often found that the system set up to exhort them to excellence wasn't really equipped to tolerate innovation. The suggestion system was used primarily in the factory, and its success was due more to a handful of prolific suggesters than to broad-based participation. In general, employees greeted management efforts to improve productivity with a fair amount of cynicism. People just did their jobs. To be sure, not all employees hesitated to come forward with ideas, and not all managers were Pattons. But the management culture generally encouraged a dominant-passive relationship between superiors and subordinates.

Several factors dissuaded me from following the Patton role model. Certainly one was that I hadn't enjoyed my own exposure to autocratic managers. But two others were more significant.

From 1974 to 1981 I headed a unit that grew from about 70 employees to 1,000. We didn't consciously choose a management style during that period of rapid growth. We didn't start from a set of assumptions that said, "This is the right way to manage our business." We experimented with all kinds of ideas. We kept the things that worked and discarded those that didn't. During those years I began to see that an ad hoc style of management could work. Perhaps we selected people who would be effective under a less rigid style of operating. For whatever reasons, the unit was very successful, and people liked working there.

Raising four children and watching them grow also influenced my thinking about participative management. I learned a great deal from my family about what people need to develop and feel happy. My family also helped me understand what values are important and showed me that a more open management style could support many of the human relations goals that I believe are important in organizational life.

Beginnings of change

These experiences persuaded me that a new management style could work in a large and complex organization. In early 1981, when I became vice president and general manager of the Defense and Marine Systems Group, I got the chance to find out for sure.

My predecessor at the group, Matt Sutton, who is now group vice president of Honeywell's other aerospace and defense group, had already made a commitment to greater employee involvement to increase productivity and improve the work climate in the organization. Quality circles of unionized hourly employees had been in place since 1978. In 1980 Matt had identified seven principles that summarized for him the way the business ought to be conducted in a people-centered management culture (see the accompanying insert). Knowing that expressing the principles was only a first step, Matt instructed his staff to translate them into practice. The project was organized under the name "Managing Today's Workforce," and a task team composed of salaried employees from all

Honeywell's new way of managing: seven principles

Productivity is a responsibility shared by management and the employee.

Broadened employee participation in decision making will be fostered.

Teamwork, mutual respect, and a sense of ownership will be promoted at all levels of the division.

Good performance is expected, and achievement will be rewarded.

A positive climate for career growth will be supported throughout the division.

The best affordable equipment and facilities required to meet job and employee needs will be provided.

Work life and personal life have interacting needs that will be recognized.

levels of the organization was formed to address each principle.

The task teams produced a rather hefty set of conditions that defined what the principles would look like in reality. But between the theory and its implementation lay a great deal of uncharted territory. There was no action plan, no sense of how we would get there from here. The findings of the seven teams had four areas in common: performance appraisal, career development, communications and involvement, and quality of work life. In 1980 we formed four teams that corresponded with these areas of concern. Simultaneously but independently, two other teams came into being, one responsible for pay and the other for equal employment opportunity and affirmative action.

Each new team was instructed to use the earlier teams' findings as a base from which to recommend specific actions. In some cases, teams' implied charters were straightforward: design a new pay system that rewards excellence and encourages high achievement; reverse the high turnover and dissatisfaction among minority employees; formalize a career development process. Other teams, however, faced ill-defined or impossibly large challenges: improve communication and employee involvement; promote quality of work life.

That some teams had to deal with issues that were overwhelming is evident only in hindsight. At the time I came into the picture, things seemed to be moving in the right direction. Within six months, many problems with this way of managing (or rather not managing) participation had become apparent. Meanwhile, we had some operational problems that needed attention as well.

For instance, we had been experiencing substantial losses in one major program that were related in part to the management culture we had developed. Over the years, we had generally stomped on the bearers of bad tidings. Naturally, no one was enthusiastic about being the messenger, so employees adapted by controlling and shaping the project information that management received. A certain amount of frenzy went on behind the scenes at lower levels to solve problems, and some serious matters were hidden from top management. The messengers were more concerned about their own survival than the survival of the project.

We quickly found that it would be in everybody's interest to develop a less confrontational management style. And people were hungry for more involvement. As the Managing Today's Workforce initiatives spread through the organization, task teams began to proliferate. Hopes were high.

Participation amok

It soon became apparent that we had no idea how many task teams we had, what problems they were addressing, how much they cost, and whether they were worth it.

In 1981 we did an inventory of the task teams, and the results gave us our first clue that the whole affair might be running amok. We counted about 200 "task teams" in existence. Some of these were actually quality circles, and we may have missed others because the people responding didn't share a common understanding of what a task team was.

Two hundred seemed a lot of teams, but we had no idea what the right number should be. Many of the teams seemed to be addressing real problems, about a third were investigating problems in the category of "interesting, but so what?" and a few teams looked like a total waste of everybody's time and effort. We had a variety of computer committees. Each building had a parking committee. Task teams and committees with overlapping jurisdictions for safety and hazardous materials abounded. No attempts to regulate duplication were made, and there was very little communication among teams.

At one point, we conducted a random survey of 39 groups and discovered that one-quarter of the participants on these teams were middle managers or above and that supervisors and managers accounted for more than half the committee time per month. Nearly half the team members came from the engineering department. Without even pulling out a calculator, we could see that the costs were enormous. We had not been managing the process at a grass-roots level. Anyone could start a task team for any reason, commandeer any combination of people, and spend any amount of time reinventing the wheel.

Nor, we soon learned, had we done an adequate job of managing the six officially sanctioned task teams. What had originally seemed like clear marching orders turned out for some teams to be equivocal. Some teams had no clear reporting relationship to the formal organization, and their charters and operating procedures were vague. Questions arose that had no clear answers. Do we make recommendations only? Or do we go ahead and implement our plans? If we don't implement them, who will? When do we report? How will we know when we've completed our work? What approvals do we need for what actions? Do we define the issue we are addressing, or must we accept the definition implicit in the work of the previous task teams? Do we have any responsibility to monitor ongoing activities that result from our recommendations? What if top management doesn't like what we recommend?

Although the task teams nominally reported to an advisory committee headed by the director of employee relations, this body had not established consistent guidelines either. Like the task teams, the advisory committee never clarified its own functions and authority or the proper direction for the general effort to increase participation.

Looking back on those early days, the following mistakes seem critical:

☐ We had set no ground rules for task teams and their chairs.

☐ We failed to clarify—to the task team managers and to the committee itself—the functions and role of the advisory committee.

☐ We did not establish accountabilities, standards, timetables, and deadlines for the task teams.

☐ The overall activity was too isolated from the main business of the division. Teams had little visibility, and employees regarded them with considerable skepticism.

☐ No common committee or mechanism linked the task teams. Attempts to avoid overlapping tasks and to communicate among teams were atypical, not part of an overall strategy.

☐ Some task team chairpersons developed too strong a sense of project ownership. "Their" programs seemed to become the team's reasons for being, and the team members were regarded as subordinates.

☐ Some teams forgot that they were supposed to represent the entire organization and that other parties had a stake in what they were doing.

☐ Some task team members complained that the time and effort absorbed by the teams seemed totally out of proportion to the impact they were having.

Two different but related problems, then, emerged from our failure to manage the new wave of participation. Teams dealing with operational issues were forming spontaneously, and many of them were out of control. We lacked what I call a coupling mechanism—we had no way to know whether teams' initiatives had an impact on the organization. For example, a task team might make terrific recommendations about new career paths, but if actually creating the paths was beyond their scope, nothing would change. In general, we didn't know if the teams were working on the right things that supported our overall business objectives, and we had no good way of finding out.

Teams working on the strategic issues had been told they were working on important issues, but they had problems: they lacked coupling mechanisms, ways of connecting what the teams did to the daily operations of the business. Working for a task team, said one member, was like wrestling with jellyfish. There was no firm substance or structure to grab onto. (See the insert "A New Way of Managing: Defining 'It.'")

We had succeeded in shaking some of the rigidity out of the organization. What we needed, we decided, was to put some discipline back in, to manage this activity with the same care and attention we give other tasks.

Putting structure in the jellyfish

The realization that we needed more structure was a real turning point for us. With the help of a consultant, we developed the concept of the parallel organization led by a steering committee. And we also decided that good business principles should apply to our participative management activities—including setting goals, defining accountabilities, and using a strategic planning approach. We began with a single steering committee for the entire business unit, which included two separate operations in Minnesota and one in Seattle. Later, after the group reorganized into divisions, we set up steering committees at each division.

The steering committee gave us a coupling mechanism, the link between the formal, hierarchical organization that carries out routine, on-going operations and the flatter, more flexible parallel organization that seeks to stimulate employee participation. The steering committee, composed of senior managers who represent the major functions of the conventional organization, ensures that concerns of the ongoing operations are reflected in the parallel organization activities and that the results of the participative problem-solving teams are incorporated into ongoing operations.

The steering committee helped overcome our previous difficulties by setting limits, objectives, and accountability for the teams; requiring the teams to make formal plans and schedules; and recognizing and rewarding the teams when their work is finished.

The employee relations department serves as staff to the steering committee; it acts as a

---

A new way of managing: defining 'it'

In 1982 Honeywell's Defense Systems Division struggled to define its new approach to management. The following excerpt appeared in a company publication:

"Other companies refer to these activities and processes by names such as QWL (quality of work life), productivity improvement, employee involvement, or participative management. But the more we thought about *all* aspects of our new way of managing, the less adequate seemed any single phrase.

"Our approach is not simply a productivity improvement program, because attention to employee needs is also important; neither is it simply a QWL effort, because we fully expect bottom-line results. Participative management is important to us, but as a *method* for achieving results, not simply as an end in itself. And all of this leaves out important ideas like 'quality' and 'innovation.'

"We used 'it' so often to stand for all these ideas that we finally decided to call it 'it.'

"This is a total way of managing our business to benefit the company, its managers, and all other employees. 'It' encompasses more than a set of particular programs. It starts with how we are organized, with a flexible structure, continually appraised for its capacity to enable people to be involved in a variety of ways and to learn and contribute from a variety of perspectives. Some areas are functionally organized, while others involve project teams from various disciplines that can work on large-scale programs.

"Cutting across the whole division is another, parallel organization for policy development and employee problem solving: the 'it' steering committee, managing a series of cross-department task teams. The 'it' steering committee consists of the divisional general manager, some members of his staff, and other key executives. The task teams it manages focus on issues such as appraisal and pay, career development, communications, quality of work life, equal employment opportunity and affirmative action, and community relations. New cross-department task teams are created periodically from employee proposals submitted to the 'it' steering committee."

liaison with the task teams, prepares them to make presentations to the steering committee, points out pitfalls, and answers routine questions and concerns. The staff also prepares briefing books for our meetings that include synopses of topics to be covered, pertinent background data, and other information that will help members use the meeting productively.

Although the steering committee meets once a month for about three hours, it may schedule longer meetings to hear task team reports. The committee also holds a day-long self-assessment about every nine months. On these occasions, outside facilitators are present to help us review our objectives and progress, examine the appropriateness of what we've done in the last period, and set priorities for the future. In short, the steering committee follows a strategic planning process with all the questions and tools that normally appear in planning for other aspects of our business.

The composition of the steering committee itself serves more than one purpose. I chair the committee because I think it's important to show that participation is not limited to the shop floor. Restricting participative management to the lower levels of the organization sends the message that this is another program to keep the natives from getting too restless, one that doesn't really reflect on "important" business. Instead, what we should be saying is "What's good for one level is good for all."

The interaction between the steering committee and the task teams has been critical to our success. Traditional taboos about who can make presentations to upper management have been removed. In relaxing our bureaucratic norms, we have increased communication between functions and levels that rarely had contact in the past. A striking illustration is a factory worker whose presentation to the steering committee eventually brought her an invitation to address the Honeywell board of directors.

Because the steering committee's role is crucial, it is important to choose the right members. They not only represent functional areas but they also play other roles. I do the selecting myself for three reasons: to signal management commitment, to facilitate the process itself, and to convert skeptics.

Because converts often become the most persuasive supporters, I chose to put skeptics on the steering committee. At first the idea threatened to backfire. Resistance was not overt, but some members could never seem to make the meetings. Partly to undercut this passive resistance, I decided to chair the committee. I could demonstrate my commitment and, at the same time, learn how the process was working and see where it needed change.

I hoped that my presence on the committee would counter the protests of other members who claimed to be too busy to attend. In a few cases, however, there was always a big business deal or customer crisis brewing somewhere else. Finally, I said, "Look, we will be meeting at this time on this day. We know you'll hate to miss the meeting, so we will arrange a teleconference. Surely you can find a telephone and participate in the meeting for an hour?" After a few teleconferences, the alternative of actually attending the meeting became much more attractive.

Attendance at steering committee meetings has become crucial because the committee provides linkages that do not exist in the formal organizational structure. Indeed, the steering committee has taken over some of the functions of traditional staff meetings, which have been abolished.

Like many organizations, the Defense and Marine Systems Group was accustomed to holding regular staff meetings, normally each Monday from 8:30 a.m. to noon. The typical format was a series of one-on-one status reports. Each staff member reported while the others sat and listened—or at least sat. I didn't believe that this was a productive use of executives' time, nor did I think that staff meetings provided an effective forum for raising important issues. Since staff meetings were regularly scheduled, people tended to hold agenda items for the meetings, and the trivial and the momentous got lumped together. In addition, people may have been reluctant to demand the general manager's time, even when such a demand was called for, if they could see him at regular meetings.

By dispensing with required staff meetings and stressing the importance of the steering committee, I think we signaled to our people that they have greater autonomy, more trust, and freer access. By breaking down the formal reporting relationship, I'm getting better reporting, while my people are getting better at handling what they need to handle and consulting when they need to consult.

The steering committee in its new form, with a clear mandate and explicit lines of authority, has proven invaluable in directing the participative effort to produce the greatest benefit to the group, its managers, and employees. We now have procedures for starting up task teams and for measuring their progress. We have means of disbanding teams once their work is done. And we have fewer task teams now. Cost is no longer a major concern because we know teams are working on important issues and will not outlive their usefulness.

Relaxing our style

Not all the efforts at changing the management culture were formally planned and executed. Many other factors contributed to a management climate more receptive to change. One of the more effective methods, I discovered, is irreverence toward some company traditions. By deliberately disregarding some habits and practices that had become entrenched in our group over the years, I think I was able to speed the transition to a more participative style.

We had to shake things up somehow. By signaling in various ways that certain traditional practices would no longer hold, we helped prepare people to accept the next idea: that they could continue to look to management to define appropriate objectives and results but they could start looking to themselves for ways of achieving them. To paraphrase our vice chairman, Jim Renier, management's role would be to set the goals and then manage the environment so people could achieve those goals. People would manage themselves.

Irreverence toward tradition can help knock down barriers to effectiveness that an organization has built up over its history. The "company way" may often obstruct productive relationships between people. One way of attacking the company way without seeming to attack the company is to demonstrate an irreverent attitude toward some hallowed customs.

One aspect of the company way at Honeywell was an excessive formality. In parts of the organization, a precisely structured chain of command was the only accepted avenue for getting things done. If a section chief had a dispute with a technical editor, he might report the incident to the chief engineer, who reported to the director of engineering, who talked with the director of marketing, who talked with the communications manager, who talked with the editorial supervisor, who talked with the technical editor, who in turn sent his response back up the chain.

We wanted to change that convention. Early on we emphasized that anyone could talk to anyone by simply dropping by the office. Then I started paying visits. At first my appearances disturbed some people who weren't used to seeing the boss unless there was bad news, but I think few people are bothered now.

I found that making ostensibly trivial adjustments to organizational life could have major repercussions. For example, soon after my arrival at the group, an issue was made of assigned parking spaces. The reorganization of which I was part increased the ranks of management. An unanticipated result was that we ended up with more managers than could be accommodated in our parking garage. When I learned that two members of my staff had flipped a coin to see who won the last available spot, I told the loser that he could have mine. Now, indoor parking may have symbolic importance in many companies, but in Minnesota in January, the symbol carries more than the usual weight.

My action sent a ripple through the executive ranks—Boyle had given up his garage space! By failing to exercise my executive prerogative, I put people on notice that we would not be operating business as usual. (Later, when a garage space did open up, I took it. But even then I did not take the number-one stall next to the door. This was another chance to send a signal that power was being used differently.)

Another manifestation of our company way was our dress habits. Although Honeywell had no strict policy on dress, house rules regarding office attire, including "mandatory" neckties, were in force throughout the organization. In the summer of 1982 I issued a memo to employees announcing a "relaxed" policy on neckties during the summer. Although I really did nothing more than restate the existing Honeywell policy, an editorial in the employee newsletter poked fun at the memo (see the *Exhibit*). Nonetheless, the editorial agreed that exercising common sense over arbitrary rules could be healthy for the organization in many areas. But only when I actually showed up at the office without a tie did people begin to believe that the new dress code was really OK.

There was little overt resistance to such changes in our organizational customs since most managers could sense which way the wind was blowing. At the corporate level, Jim Renier's emphatic support of cultural change gave our efforts added strength. However, some managers in other parts of the company and some of our customers who had entrusted us with large projects expressed strong reservations about what we were doing. They were not sure that an irreverent management could be a serious and effective management. The company way held that schedule and cost control resulted from bearing down on people and not letting up until they screamed. Customers were concerned with results, not symbols. But when we were able to demonstrate performance improvement—in some cases, remarkable improvement in quality, yields, and learning curves—our customers came around.

Return on the investment

I don't mean to suggest that we have solved every problem. Sometimes we accept solutions that are less than optimal or we live through the protracted birth of something that could have been handled quickly and simply by one person. On the other hand, our new system is more likely to produce answers that seemed totally out of reach in the past. Let me offer some examples.

Our career development task team took two-and-one-half years to generate a career development program for employees. We could have brought in a consultant for the money we spent internally and probably have had a similar program in one-fifth the time. But having a program isn't sufficient. Once it's in place, supervisors and employees must understand it, accept it, and be willing to use it. Putting up with contending factions agonizing over a solution was worth the quick and full acceptance of the result later on.

One of the hardest things about becoming a more participative manager is the occasional need to sacrifice the best solution or approach to a problem to sustain employee involvement. People who are always turned down will eventually become turned off. For example, our pay task team introduced a new salary program based on performance improvement and tied to specific markets. The new method of determining pay raises eliminated many inequities from the old system, clarified when and how raises would be delivered, and rewarded people fairly based on their improved performance. The team's ongoing role included monitoring the system and fine-tuning it as we learned how well it was working.

After one year both the team members and supervisory personnel felt that the program worked very well, except for one problem: How should we deal with experienced employees whose work was unlikely to improve in the future? These employees, primarily senior engineers, were important contributors; nevertheless, they were ineligible for merit salary increases because the system rewarded performance improvement, not performance level. The lack of merit pay was discouraging people we didn't want to discourage, the team argued, because we seemed to be saying that their work was not valuable. The task team wanted to add a feature to the system called "lump-sum merit." This would enable supervisors to reward these steady but valued workers.

At the time, I disagreed with the task team and argued that the steady employees were already highly paid for their competence, that lump-sum merit would open up a whole new range of problems, and that the team was applying a Band-Aid to avoid reexamining the entire system. The steering committee rejected the proposal on two occasions. Yet the team presented a third refinement of the lump-sum merit scheme. This time team members were adamant, and they were also beginning to grumble that participative management would be condoned only as long as it produced what top management was looking for. The compensation team was one of the best we had, and I was alienating its members from the process through which they had performed so well. Eventually I decided that it would be better to support the proposal and deal with the consequences later than to fur-

Exhibit   **The necktie flap**

Honeywell Interoffice Correspondence

Date: May 10, 1982
Subject: LOOSENING UP THE TIE

To: All DSD Minneapolis   From: R. J. Boyle
    Salaried Employees   Organization: DSD-Hopkins
                                        HED: MN11
                                        MS: 2010
                                        HVN: 931-6500

To conserve energy, thermostat settings are higher in the summer and lower in the winter than previously experienced. To compensate, more comfortable clothing appropriate to the summer season in Minnesota will help make the working environment more pleasant and comfortable.

I wish to announce a relaxed wearing apparel policy, and loosen my tie for the summer. Let's try it starting on May 15th and tentatively ending on September 15th. Since departments vary in customer contact and, depending on location, may even vary slightly in temperature, Department Heads are hereby given authority to allow variations.

Wearing apparel and other facets of personal appearance will remain a matter of individual employee choice providing the following conditions exist:

1. A safety hazard is not created for the employee or other employees.

2. There is no demonstrable adverse affect on the ability of the individual or other employees to perform their jobs.

3. Both wearing apparel and personal appearance must be in keeping with the working and business atmosphere of the area.

4. When meeting with customers or vendors who do not have a relaxed dress code, or when representing the company in any way where a casual image would be inappropriate, this relaxation does not apply.

This change requires each of us to use good judgement. On the one extreme it means you do not have to wear a tie; on the other tennis shoes, shorts and a t-shirt is too relaxed. Have a comfortable, enjoyable summer. I hope to.

R.J. Boyle

R.J. Boyle

RJB:bjh

81-3386-128 (Rev. 6-80)

Another way to save energy

Dressing for the occasion is merely good corporate sense. You dress up for dealing with customers. You dress down for dealing with a leaky screw machine. You loosen your collar to improve the flow of blood to your brain.

We know these things without being told. We do them without realizing that we are making choices.

So why is our leader making a big deal out of loosening ties when it gets warm? Why is he announcing a "relaxed wearing apparel policy" that is the same one we've had for years?

Now, the trouble with being a Dick Boyle is that everyone dresses up when they have to meet you. It might be easy to imagine the workforce is chronically overdressed when you see a daily parade of people in prom clothes.

But there's something else going on here. It's a quiet way of saying that the way things have always been isn't necessarily the way they have to be.

To illustrate, examine the next random gathering of managers in your vicinity. Count the number of managers. Then count the number of white shirts.

Are white shirts part of the job description? No. Are they coincidence? No.

House rules.

House rules are unwritten rules that everyone figures must be written down somewhere, since everyone follows them. In some departments, to wear a golf shirt is an act of courage. In others, a suit is an invitation to curiosity, if not outright hooting.

So the great tie memo, while maybe seeming trivial to some people, was a declaration of freedom to others. It said that we don't have to do things just because we've always done them. Look at the situation, and if there's a reason for wearing a strip of cloth knotted around your windpipe, then do it.

But if it has only been custom that dictates a tie (or white shirt or black pumps), we have a choice in the matter. Some people will still feel more productive wearing a jacket. Others will charge their batteries by rolling up their sleeves.

Unspoken rules and customs will always weigh heavily on behavior in the organization. Selecting what to wear to work is certainly not the most important place we let conventional thinking prematurely limit our options. So maybe it *is* worth a reminder from the top to work smarter, not hotter....

Charlie Quimby

ther alienate them—and probably many others with whom they had contact.

The proposal had one more hurdle to clear. Because numerous Honeywell divisions are located in the Minneapolis area, corporate approval is required for compensation programs to ensure consistency among these operations. In the end, corporate staff rejected our lump-sum merit proposal. Although they lost, the team members achieved a moral victory. The process worked. The process, in this case, was more important than the product.

The limited numbers of women and minority people in our group was another problem that concerned many of us. Our EEO data were unambiguous: whatever we might claim about our organization, we had limited success in hiring and retaining minority employees and we couldn't seem to find better answers. We had EEO standards in our contracts and in our division and departmental objectives, but we were having difficulty reaching our goals. Our retention rate highlighted the problem. In 1980, we lost seven minority employees for every ten we hired. Simply issuing an order to hire minorities was not having the desired effect.

An EEO task team composed of middle managers was formed to attack the problem. To their credit, the members looked around the table and saw nothing but white, middle-aged male faces, and they began to see the situation in a new light. The team voted to add minority members, and the original group received an eye-opening education in race relations. One manager admitted that he didn't know that blacks weren't calling themselves negroes anymore. The team learned firsthand about the difficulties that face young black engineers from southern schools who move to predominantly white Minnesota and find the weather, the culture, and the company unfriendly.

To deal with such problems, the team eventually developed a comprehensive EEO affirmative action plan, a training program in cultural awareness for supervisors, a minority scholarship program, a career development program, and an appeals process.

We still need to improve opportunities for minorities, women, and handicapped workers at Honeywell Defense and Marine Systems. But the climate of our operations has improved dramatically, and the minority retention rate has improved threefold to be in line with the rate for the work force generally.

Finally, the participative process can pay off by solving problems beyond the ones addressed directly. Recently I was faced with a management decision that in the past I would have made on my own. Two of the group's major units had cooperated to win a very large contract. The project would require the skills of both units, but the production could take place in only one. Thus, one unit would receive a very large flow of revenues. This unit would also receive a large amount of capital improvement funds. To make matters worse, the two units had been extremely competitive with each other over the years. The capital investments flowing to one of them would give it an edge for years to come.

Rather than deciding between the units myself, I involved both units in the decision. Over six months, I met with the directors of the units and their staffs periodically to discuss alternative approaches and the implications of winning and losing. Members of both units had the opportunity to argue their case, and each side heard the other's views and concerns. Getting these units to share data was an accomplishment in itself in light of their long-standing rivalry.

In the end, we concluded that the winning unit might have to subsidize the losing unit for some time. During these discussions, members of both units began to develop a clearer vision of long-range corporate goals and began to see these as distinct from the goals of their own units.

Each unit still favored its own case. But when I made the final decision in favor of one, the losing side did not go into a blue funk. Everyone understood the reasons for the decison. The winning team was also smart enough not to gloat. The project proceeded smoothly because we had anticipated many of the potential snags. Finally, the two units developed a cooperative relationship for the first time that really benefits the group as a whole. In fact, a few months ago I discovered that one of the units had voluntarily relinquished control over a project to the other without involving me in the decision.

With participative management yielding such benefits, I am able to work on other management concerns. Although I spend more time managing participation, I spend less time refereeing internal squabbles or soothing irate customers. Our employees are solving little problems before they become big problems. Many more decisions are made at lower levels of the organization. Anything they want to keep out of my office is fine with me.

Participative management does require a greater commitment of time compared with traditional management intervention, at least in the short term. But the long-term rewards of *managed* participative management are abundant. Not the least of them is the fun I'm having doing my job.

Reprint 84103

We don't need flat organizations. We need layers of accountability and skill.

In Praise of Hierarchy

by Elliott Jaques

At first glance, hierarchy may seem difficult to praise. Bureaucracy is a dirty word even among bureaucrats, and in business there is a widespread view that managerial hierarchy kills initiative, crushes creativity, and has therefore seen its day. Yet 35 years of research have convinced me that managerial hierarchy is the most efficient, the hardiest, and in fact the most natural structure ever devised for large organizations. Properly structured, hierarchy can release energy and creativity, rationalize productivity, and actually improve morale. Moreover, I think most managers know this intuitively and have only lacked a workable structure and a decent intellectual justification for what they have always known could work and work well.

As presently practiced, hierarchy undeniably has its drawbacks. One of business's great contemporary problems is how to release and sustain among the people who work in corporate hierarchies the thrust, initiative, and adaptability of the entrepreneur. This problem is so great that it has become fashionable to call for a new kind of organization to put in place of managerial hierarchy, an organization that will better meet the requirements of what is variously called the Information Age, the Services Age, or the Post-Industrial Age.

As vague as the description of the age is the definition of the kind of new organization required to suit it. Theorists tell us it ought to look more like a symphony orchestra or a hospital or perhaps the British raj. It ought to function by means of primus groups or semiautonomous work teams or matrix overlap groups. It should be organic or entrepreneurial or tight-loose. It should hinge on skunk works or on management by walking around or perhaps on our old friend, management by objective.

All these approaches are efforts to overcome the perceived faults of hierarchy and find better ways to improve morale and harness human creativity. But the theorists' belief that our changing world requires an alternative to hierarchical organization is simply wrong, and all their proposals are based on an inadequate understanding of not only hierarchy but also human nature.

Hierarchy is not to blame for our problems. Encouraged by gimmicks and fads masquerading as insights, we have burdened our managerial systems with a makeshift scaffolding of inept structures and attitudes. What we need is not simply a new, flatter organization but an understanding of how managerial hierarchy functions—how it relates to the complexity of work and how we can use it to achieve a more effective deployment of talent and energy.

The reason we have a hierarchical organization of work is not only that tasks occur in lower and higher degrees of complexity—which is obvious—but also that there are sharp discontinuities in complexity that separate tasks into a series of steps or categories—which is not so obvious. The same discontinuities occur with respect to mental work and to the breadth and duration of accountability. The hierarchical kind of organization we call bureaucracy did not emerge accidentally. It is the only form of

> **Managerial hierarchy has never been properly described or adequately used.**

organization that can enable a company to employ large numbers of people and yet preserve unambiguous accountability for the work they do. And that is why, despite its problems, it has so doggedly persisted.

Elliott Jaques, currently visiting research professor in management science at George Washington University, has been studying hierarchy and organizational structure for 40 years. His most recent book is Requisite Organization: The CEO's Guide to Creative Structure and Leadership *(Cason Hall/Gower, 1989).*

Hierarchy has not had its day. Hierarchy never did have its day. As an organizational system, managerial hierarchy has never been adequately described and has just as certainly never been adequately used. The problem is not to find an alternative to a system that once worked well but no longer does; the problem is to make it work efficiently for the first time in its 3,000-year history.

What Went Wrong...

There is no denying that hierarchical structure has been the source of a great deal of trouble and inefficiency. Its misuse has hampered effective management and stifled leadership, while it's track record as a support for entrepreneurial energy has not been exemplary. We might almost say that successful businesses have had to succeed despite hierarchical organization rather than because of it.

One common complaint is excessive layering—too many rungs on the ladder. Information passes through too many people, decisions through too many levels, and managers and subordinates are too close together in experience and ability, which smothers effective leadership, cramps accountability, and promotes buck passing. Relationships grow stressful when managers and subordinates bump elbows, so to speak, within the same frame of reference.

Another frequent complaint is that few managers seem to add real value to the work of their subordinates. The fact that the breakup value of many large corporations is greater than their share value shows pretty clearly how much value corporate managers can *subtract* from their subsidiary businesses, but in fact few of us know exactly what managerial added value would look like as it was occurring.

Many people also complain that our present hierarchies bring out the nastier aspects of human behavior, like greed, insensitivity, careerism, and self-importance. These are the qualities that have sent many behavioral scientists in search of cooperative, group-oriented, nonhierarchical organizational forms. But are they the inevitable companions of hierarchy, or perhaps a product of the misuse of hierarchy that would disappear if hierarchy were properly understood and structured?

...And What Continues to Go Wrong

The fact that so many of hierarchy's problems show up in the form of individual misbehavior has led to one of the most widespread illusions in business, namely, that a company's managerial leadership can be significantly improved solely by doing psychotherapeutic work on the personalities and attitudes of its managers. Such methods can help individuals gain greater personal insight, but I doubt that individual insight, personality matching, or even exercises in group dynamics can produce much in the way of organizational change or an overall improvement in leadership effectiveness. The problem is that our managerial hierarchies are so badly designed as to defeat the best efforts even of psychologically insightful individuals.

Solutions that concentrate on groups, on the other hand, fail to take into account the real nature of employment systems. People are not employed in groups. They are employed individually, and their employment contracts—real or implied—are individual. Group members may insist in moments of great esprit de corps that the group as such is the author of some particular accomplishment, but once the work is completed, the members of the group look for individual recognition and individual progression in

> **No one ever holds groups accountable for their work. Who ever heard of promoting a group—or firing one?**

their careers. And it is not groups but individuals whom the company will hold accountable. The only true group is the board of directors, with its corporate liability.

None of the group-oriented panaceas face this issue of accountability. All the theorists refer to group authority, group decisions, and group consensus, none of them to group accountability. Indeed, they avoid the issue of accountability altogether, for to hold a group accountable, the employment contract would have to be with the group, not with the individuals, and companies simply do not employ groups as such.

To understand hierarchy, you must first understand employment. To be employed is to have an ongoing contract that holds you accountable for doing work of a given type for a specified number of hours per week in exchange for payment. Your specific tasks within that given work are assigned to you by a person called your manager (or boss or supervisor), who *ought to be held accountable* for the work you do.

If we are to make our hierarchies function properly, it is essential to place the emphasis on *accountability for getting work done*. This is what hierarchical systems ought to be about. Authority is a secondary issue and flows from accountability in the sense that there should be just that amount of authority needed to discharge the accountability. So if a group is to be given authority, its members must be held accountable as a group, and unless this is done, it is very hard to take so-called group decisions seriously. If the CEO or the manager of the group is held accountable for outcomes, then in the final analysis, he or she will have to agree with group decisions or have the authority to block them, which means that the group never really had decision-making power to begin with. Alternatively, if groups are allowed to make decisions without their manager's seal of approval, then accountability as such will suffer, for if a group does badly, the group is never fired. (And it would be shocking if it were.)

In the long run, therefore, group authority *without* group accountability is dysfunctional, and group authority *with* group accountability is unacceptable. So images of organizations that are more like symphony orchestras or hospitals or the British raj are surely nothing more than metaphors to express a desired feeling of togetherness—the togetherness produced by a conductor's baton, the shared concern of doctors and nurses for their patients, or the apparent unity of the British civil service in India.

In employment systems, after all, people are not mustered to play together as their manager beats time. As for hospitals, they are the essence of everything bad about bureaucratic organization. They function in spite of the system, only because of the enormous professional devotion of their staffs. The Indian civil service was in many ways like a hospital, its people bound together by the struggle to survive in a hostile environment. Managers do need authority, but authority based appropriately on the accountabilities they must discharge.

Why Hierarchy?

The bodies that govern companies, unions, clubs, and nations all employ people to do work, and they all organize these employees in managerial hierarchies, systems that allow organizations to hold people accountable for getting assigned work done. Unfortunately, we often lose sight of this goal and set up the organizational layers in our managerial hierarchies to accommodate pay brackets and facilitate career development instead. If work happens to get done as well, we consider that a useful bonus.

But if our managerial hierarchical organizations tend to choke so readily on debilitating bureaucratic practices, how do we explain the persistence and continued spread of this form of organization for more than 3,000 years? And why has the determined search for alternatives proved so fruitless?

The answer is that managerial hierarchy is and will remain the *only* way to structure unified working systems with hundreds, thousands, or tens of thousands of employees, for the very good reason that managerial hierarchy is the expression of two fundamental characteristics of real work. First, the tasks we carry out are not only more or less complex but they also become more complex as they separate out into discrete categories or types of complexity. Second, the same is true of the mental work that people do on the job, for as this work grows more complex, it too separates out into distinct categories or types of mental activity. In turn, these two characteristics permit hierarchy to meet four of any organization's fundamental needs: to add real value to work as it moves through the organization, to identify and nail down accountability at each stage of the value-adding process, to place people with the necessary competence at each organizational layer, and to build a general consensus and acceptance of the managerial structure that achieves these ends.

Hierarchical Layers

The complexity of the problems encountered in a particular task, project, or strategy is a function of the variables involved—their number, their clarity or ambiguity, the rate at which they change, and, overall, the extent to which they are distinct or tangled. Obviously, as you move higher in a managerial hierarchy, the most difficult problems you have to contend with become increasingly complex. The biggest problems faced by the CEO of a large corporation are vastly more complex than those encountered on the shop floor. The CEO must cope not only with a huge array of often amorphous and constantly changing data but also with variables so tightly interwoven that they must be disentangled before they will yield useful information. Such variables might include the cost of capital, the interplay of corporate cash flow, the structure of the international competitive market, the uncertainties of Europe after 1992, the future of Pacific Rim development, social developments with respect to labor, political developments in Eastern Europe, the Middle East, and the Third World, and technological research and change.

That the CEO's and the lathe operator's problems are different in quality as well as quantity will come as no surprise to anyone. The question is—and always has been—where does the change in quality occur? On a continuum of complexity from the bottom of the structure to the top, where are the discontinuities that will allow us to identify layers of hierarchy that are distinct and separable, as different as ice is from water and water from steam? I spent years looking for the answer, and what I found was somewhat unexpected.

My first step was to recognize the obvious, that the layers have to do with manager-subordinate relationships. The manager's position is in one layer and the subordinate's is in the next layer below. What then sets the necessary distance between? This question cannot be answered without knowing just what it is that a manager does.

The managerial role has three critical features. First, and *most* critical, every manager must be held accountable not only for the work of subordinates but also for adding value to their work. Second, every manager must be held accountable for sustaining a team of subordinates capable of doing this work. Third, every manager must be held accountable for setting direction and getting subordinates to follow willingly, indeed enthusiastically. In brief, every manager is accountable for work and leadership.

In order to make accountability possible, managers must have enough authority to ensure that their subordinates can do the work assigned to them. This authority must include at least these four elements: (1) the right to veto any applicant who, in the manager's opinion, falls below the minimum standards of ability; (2) the power to make work assignments; (3) the power to carry out performance appraisals and, within the limits of company policy, to make decisions—not recommendations—about raises and merit rewards; and (4) the authority to initiate removal—at least from the manager's own team—of anyone who seems incapable of doing the work.

But defining the basic nature of the managerial role reveals only part of what a managerial layer means. It cannot tell us how wide a managerial layer should be, what the difference in responsibility should be between a manager and a subordinate, or, most important, where the break should come between one managerial layer and another. Fortunately, the next step in the research process supplied the missing piece of the puzzle.

Responsibility and Time

This second step was the unexpected and startling discovery that the level of responsibility in any organizational role—whether a manager's or an individual contributor's—can be objectively measured in terms of the target completion time of the *longest* task, project, or program assigned to that role. The more distant the target completion date of the longest task or program, the heavier the weight of responsibility is felt to be. I call this measure the responsibility time span of the role. For example, a supervisor whose principal job is to plan tomorrow's production assignments and next week's work schedule but who also has ongoing responsibility for uninterrupted production supplies for the month ahead has a responsibility time span of one month. A foreman who spends most of his time riding herd on

> **Hierarchical layers depend on jumps in responsibility that depend in turn on how far ahead a manager must think and plan.**

this week's production quotas but who must also develop a program to deal with the labor requirements of next year's retooling has a responsibility time span of a year or a little more. The advertising vice president who stays late every night working on next week's layouts but who also has to begin making contingency plans for the expected launch of two new local advertising media campaigns three years hence has a responsibility time span of three years.

To my great surprise, I found that in all types of managerial organizations in many different countries over 35 years, people in roles at the same time span experience the same weight of responsibility and declare the same level of pay to be fair, regardless of their occupation or actual pay. The time-span range runs from a day at the bottom of a large corporation to more than 20 years at the top, while the felt-fair pay ranges from $15,000 to $1 million and more.

Armed with my definition of a manager and my time-span measuring instrument, I then bumped into the second surprising finding—repeatedly confirmed—about layering in managerial hierarchies: the boundaries between successive managerial layers occur at certain specific time-span increments, just as ice changes to water and water to steam at certain specific temperatures. And the fact that everyone in the hierarchy, regardless of status, seems to see these boundaries in the same places suggests that the boundaries reflect some universal truth about human nature.

The illustration "Managerial Hierarchy in Fiction and in Fact" shows the hierarchical structure of

Managerial Hierarchy in Fiction and in Fact

```
         7½ years
  Ⓐ ─────────────────────────────  Ⓐ
        5 ─────────────────────┐
  Ⓑ ─────────────────────── Ⓑ  │
        4 ─────────────────────┤
  Ⓒ ─────────────────────── Ⓒ  │
        3 ─────────────────────┤
  Ⓓ ─────────────────────── Ⓓ
        2
  Hierarchy              Hierarchy
  according to           according to
  the organization       the people
  chart
```

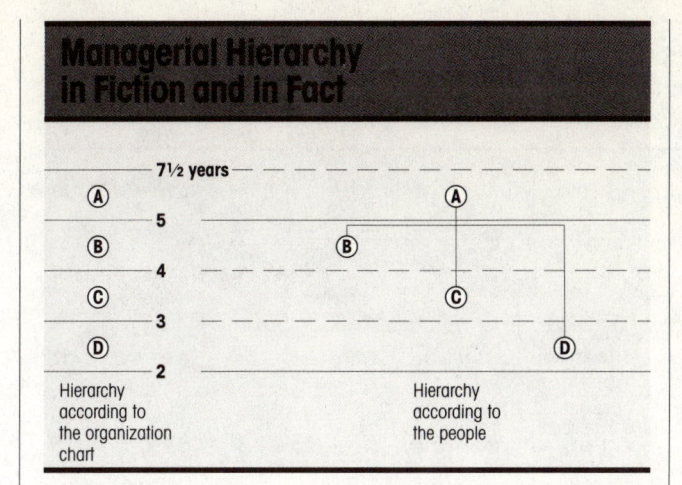

part of a department at one company I studied, along with the approximate responsibility time span for each position. The longest task for manager A was more than five years, while for B, C, and D, the longest tasks fell between two and five years. Note also that according to the organization chart, A is the designated manager of B, B of C, and C of D.

In reality, the situation was quite different. Despite the managerial roles specified by the company, B, C, and D all described A as their "real" boss. C complained that B was "far too close" and "breathing down my neck." D had the same complaint about C. B and C also admitted to finding it very difficult to manage their immediate subordinates, C and D respectively, who seemed to do better if treated as colleagues and left alone.

In short, there appeared to be a cutoff at five years, such that those with responsibility time spans of less than five years felt they needed a manager with a responsibility time span of more than five years. Manager D, with a time span of two to three years, did not feel that C, with a time span of three to four, was distant enough hierarchically to take orders from. D felt the same way about B. Only A filled the bill for *any* of the other three.

As the responsibility time span increased in the example from two years to three to four and approached five, no one seemed to perceive a qualitative difference in the nature of the responsibility that a manager discharged. Then, suddenly, when a manager had responsibility for tasks and projects that exceeded five years in scope, everyone seemed to perceive a difference not only in the scope of responsibility but also in its quality and in the kind of work and worker required to discharge it.

I found several such discontinuities that appeared consistently in more than 100 studies. Real managerial and hierarchical boundaries occur at time spans of three months, one year, two years, five years, ten years, and twenty years.

These natural discontinuities in our perception of the responsibility time span create hierarchical strata that people in different companies, countries, and circumstances all seem to regard as genuine and acceptable. The existence of such boundaries has important implications in nearly every sphere of organizational management. One of these is performance appraisal. Another is the capacity of managers to add value to the work of their subordinates.

The only person with the perspective and authority to judge and communicate personal effectiveness is an employee's accountable manager, who, in most cases, is also the only person from whom an employee will accept evaluation and coaching. This accountable manager must be the supervisor one real layer higher in the hierarchy, not merely the next higher employee on the pay scale.

As I suggested earlier, part of the secret to making hierarchy work is to distinguish carefully between hierarchical layers and pay grades. The trouble is that companies need two to three times as many pay grades as they do working layers, and once they've established the pay grades, which are easy to describe and set up, they fail to take the next step and set up a different managerial hierarchy based on responsibility rather than salary. The result is too many layers.

My experience with organizations of all kinds in many different countries has convinced me that effective value-adding managerial leadership of subordinates can come only from an individual one category higher in cognitive capacity, working one category higher in problem complexity. By contrast, wherever managers and subordinates are in the same layer—separated only by pay grade—subordinates see the boss as too close, breathing down their necks, and they identify their "real" boss as the next manager at a genuinely higher level of cognitive and task complexity. This kind of overlayering is what produces the typical symptoms of bureaucracy in its worst form—too much passing problems up and down the system, bypassing, poor task setting, frustrated subordinates, anxious managers, wholly inadequate performance appraisals, "personality problems" everywhere, and so forth.

Layering at Company X

Companies need more than seven pay grades—as a rule, many more. But seven hierarchical layers is enough or more than enough for all but the largest corporations.

Let me illustrate this pattern of hierarchical layering with the case of two divisions of Company X, a corporation with 32,000 employees and annual sales of $7 billion. As shown in "Two Divisions of Corporation X," the CEO sets strategic goals that look ahead as far as 25 years and manages executive vice presidents with responsibility for 12- to 15-year development programs. One vice president is accountable for several strategic business units, each with a president who works with critical tasks of up to 7 years duration.

One of these units (Y Products) employs 2,800 people, has annual sales of $250 million, and is engaged in the manufacture and sale of engineering products, with traditional semiskilled shop-floor production at Layer I. The other unit (Z Press) publishes books and employs only 88 people. Its funding and negotiations with authors are in the hands of a general editor at Layer IV, assisted by a small group of editors at Layer III, each working on projects that may take up to 18 months to complete.

So the president of Y Products manages more people, governs a greater share of corporate resources, and earns a lot more money for the parent company than does the president of Z Press. Yet the two presidents occupy the same hierarchical layer, have similar authority, and take home comparable salaries. This is neither coincidental nor unfair. It is natural, correct, and efficient.

It is the level of responsibility, *measured in terms of time span*, that tells you how many layers you need in an enterprise—not the number of subordinates or the magnitude of sales or profits. These factors may have a marginal influence on salary; they have no bearing at all on hierarchical layers.

Changes in the Quality of Work

The widespread and striking consistency of this underlying pattern of true managerial layers leads naturally to the question of why it occurs. Why do people perceive a sudden leap in status from, say, four-and-a-half years to five and from nine to ten?

The answer goes back to the earlier discussion of complexity. As we go higher in a managerial hierarchy, the most difficult problems that arise grow increasingly complex, and, as the complexity of a task increases, so does the complexity of the mental work required to handle it. What I found when I looked at this problem over the course of ten years was that this complexity, like responsibility time span, also occurs in leaps or jumps. In other words, the most difficult tasks found within any given layer are all characterized by the same type or category of complexity, just as water remains in the same liquid state from 0° to 100° Celsius, even though it ranges from very cold to very hot. (A few degrees cooler or hotter and water changes in state, to ice or steam.)

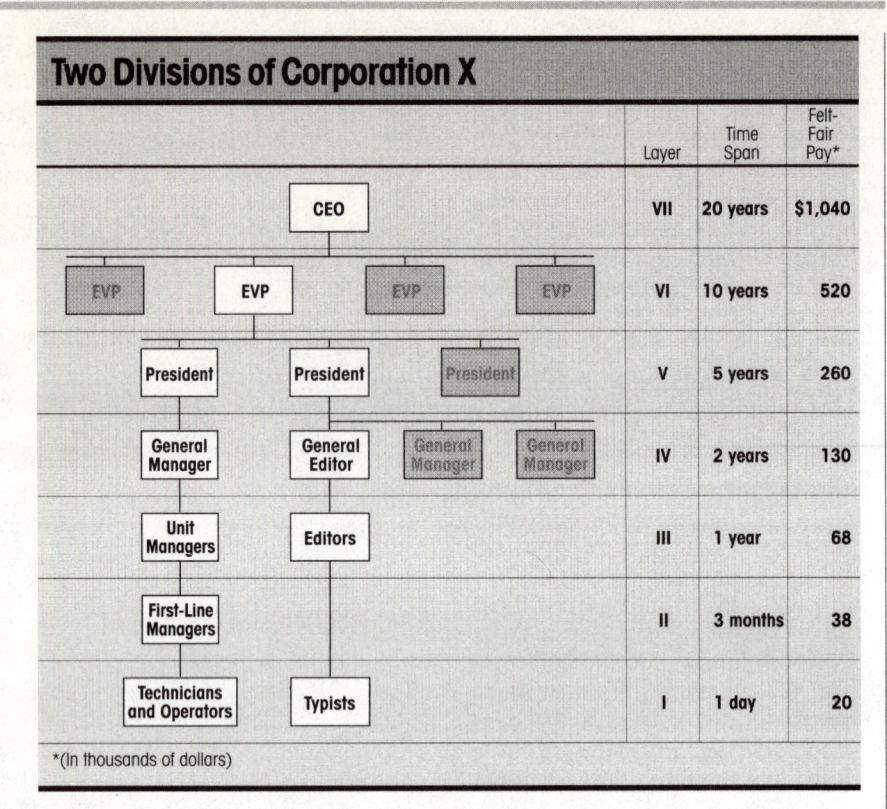

It is this suddenly increased level of necessary mental capacity, experience, knowledge, and mental stamina that allows managers to add value to the work of their subordinates. What they add is a new perspective, one that is broader, more experienced, and, most important, one that extends further in time. If, at Z Press, the editors at Layer III find and develop manuscripts into books with market potential, it is their general editor at Layer IV who fits those books into the press's overall list, who thinks ahead to their position on next year's list and later allocates resources to their production and marketing, and who makes projections about the publishing and book-buying trends of the next two to five years.

It is also this sudden change in the quality, not just the quantity, of managerial work that subordinates accept as a natural and appropriate break in the con-

Two Divisions of Corporation X

	Layer	Time Span	Felt-Fair Pay*
CEO	VII	20 years	$1,040
EVP	VI	10 years	520
President	V	5 years	260
General Manager / General Editor	IV	2 years	130
Unit Managers / Editors	III	1 year	68
First-Line Managers	II	3 months	38
Technicians and Operators / Typists	I	1 day	20

*(In thousands of dollars)

tinuum of hierarchy. It is why they accept the boss's authority and not just the boss's power.

So the whole picture comes together. Managerial hierarchy or layering is the only effective organizational form for deploying people and tasks at complementary levels, where people can do the tasks assigned to them, where the people in any given layer can add value to the work of those in the layer below them, and, finally, where this stratification of management strikes everyone as necessary and welcome.

What we need is not some new kind of organization. What we need is managerial hierarchy that understands its own nature and purpose. Hierarchy is the best structure for getting work done in big organizations. Trying to raise efficiency and morale without first setting this structure to rights is like trying to lay bricks without mortar. No amount of exhortation, attitudinal engineering, incentive planning, or even leadership will have any permanent effect unless we understand what hierarchy is and why and how it works. We need to stop casting about fruitlessly for organizational Holy Grails and settle down to the hard work of putting our managerial hierarchies in order.

Reprint 90107

"Let's not panic until we see how the Fed reacts."

Participation on the Factory Floor

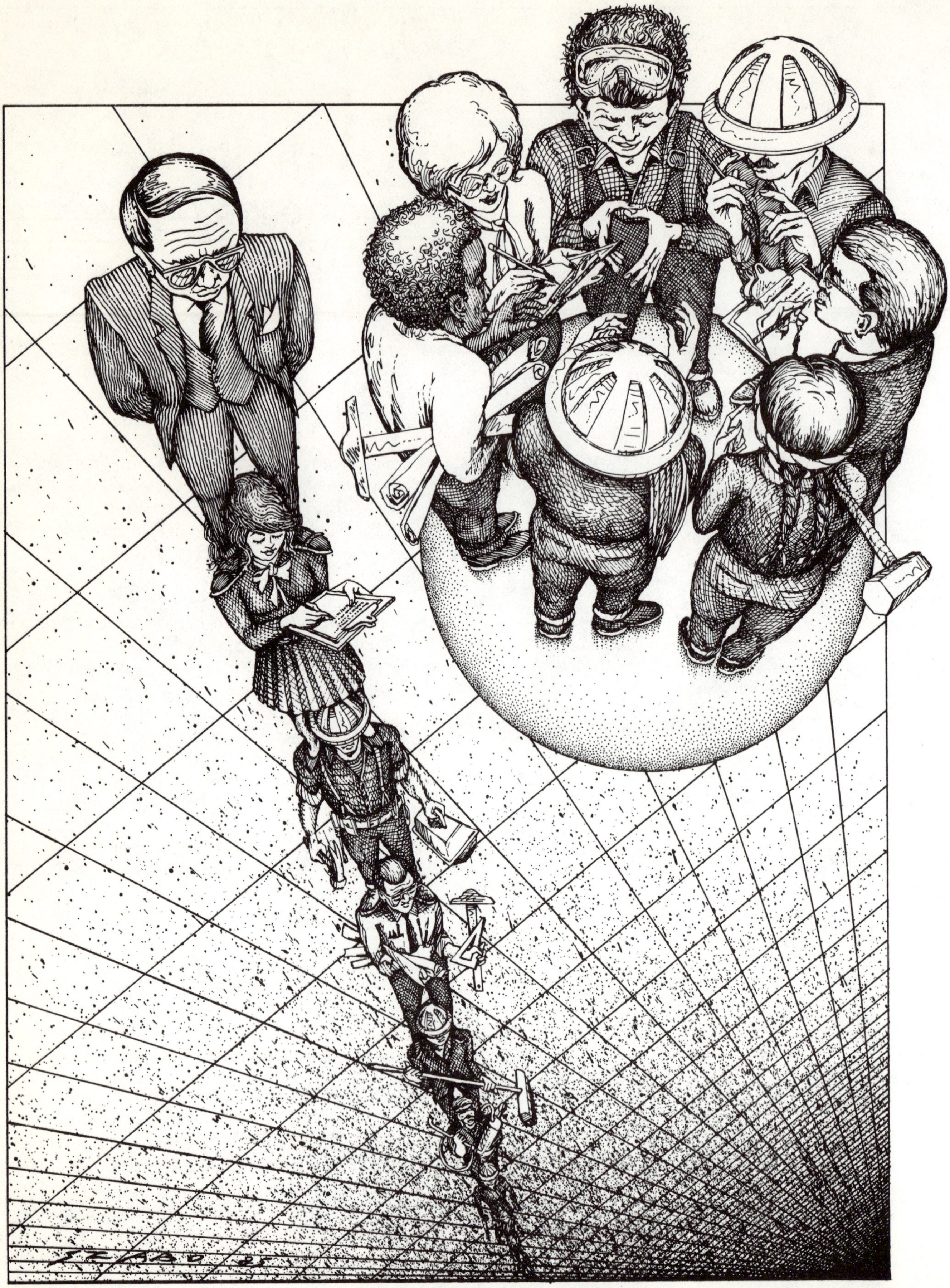

Richard E. Walton

From control to commitment in the workplace

In factory after factory, there is a revolution under way in the management of work

The symptoms are familiar: a good strategy is not executed well; costs rise out of all proportion to gains in productivity; high rates of absenteeism persist; and a disaffected work force, taking little pride or pleasure in what it does, retards innovation and quality improvements. To those at the top of the corporate ladder, it seems as if they are the captains of a ship in which the wheel is not connected to the rudder. Whatever decisions get made, little happens down below. Only lately have managers themselves begun to take responsibility for these symptoms and for the approach to work-force management out of which they grow. Only lately have they begun to see that workers respond best – and most creatively – not when they are tightly controlled by management, placed in narrowly defined jobs, and treated like an unwelcome necessity, but, instead, when they are given broader responsibilities, encouraged to contribute, and helped to take satisfaction in their work. It should come as no surprise that eliciting worker commitment – and providing the environment in which it can flourish – pays tangible dividends for the individuals and for the company. The author describes these opposing approaches to a company's human capital and points out the key challenges in moving from one to the other.

Mr. Walton, Jesse Isidore Straus Professor of Business Administration at the Harvard Business School, is a recognized authority on issues related to work-force management. His prior articles in HBR include "Improving the Quality of Work Life" (May-June 1974) and "Work Innovations in the United States" (July-August 1979). For some time now, his research interests have addressed the evolution of the "commitment model" discussed in this article.

Illustration by Gustav Szabo.

The larger shape of institutional change is always difficult to recognize when one stands right in the middle of it. Today, throughout American industry, a significant change is under way in long-established approaches to the organization and management of work. Although this shift in attitude and practice takes a wide variety of company-specific forms, its larger shape – its overall pattern – is already visible if one knows where and how to look.

Consider, for example, the marked differences between two plants in the chemical products division of a major U.S. corporation. Both make similar products and employ similar technologies, but that is virtually all they have in common.

The first, organized by businesses with an identifiable product or product line, divides its employees into self-supervising 10- to 15-person work teams that are collectively responsible for a set of related tasks. Each team member has the training to perform many or all of the tasks for which the team is accountable, and pay reflects the level of mastery of required skills. These teams have received assurances that management will go to extra lengths to provide continued employment in any economic downturn. The teams have also been thoroughly briefed on such issues as market share, product costs, and their implications for the business.

Not surprisingly, this plant is a top performer economically and rates well on all measures of employee satisfaction, absenteeism, turnover, and safety. With its employees actively engaged in identifying and solving problems, it operates with fewer levels of management and fewer specialized departments than do its sister plants. It is also one of the principal suppliers of management talent for these other plants and for the division manufacturing staff.

In the second plant, each employee is responsible for a fixed job and is required to perform up to the minimum standard defined for that job. Peer pressure keeps new employees from exceeding the minimum standards and from taking other initiatives that go beyond basic job requirements. Supervisors, who manage daily assignments and monitor performance, have long since given up hope for anything more than compliance with standards, finding sufficient difficulty in getting their people to perform adequately most of the time. In fact, they and their workers try to prevent the industrial engineering department, which is under pressure from top plant management to improve operations, from using changes in methods to "jack up" standards.

A recent management campaign to document an "airtight case" against employees who have excessive absenteeism or sub-par performance mirrors employees' low morale and high distrust of management. A constant stream of formal grievances, violations of plant rules, harassment of supervisors, wildcat walkouts, and even sabotage has prevented the plant from reaching its productivity and quality goals and has absorbed a disproportionate amount of division staff time. Dealings with the union are characterized by contract negotiations on economic matters and skirmishes over issues of management control.

No responsible manager, of course, would ever wish to encourage the kind of situation at this second plant, yet the determination to understand its deeper causes and to attack them at their root does not come easily. Established modes of doing things have an inertia all their own. Such an effort is, however, in process all across the industrial landscape. And with that effort comes the possibility of a revolution in industrial relations every bit as great as that occasioned by the rise of mass production the better part of a century ago. The challenge is clear to those managers willing to see it – and the potential benefits, enormous.

Approaches to work-force management

What explains the extraordinary differences between the plants just described? Is it that the first is new (built in 1976) and the other old? Yes and no. Not all new plants enjoy so fruitful an approach to work organization; not all older plants have such intractable problems. Is it that one plant is unionized and the other not? Again, yes and no. The presence of a union may institutionalize conflict and lackluster performance, but it seldom causes them.

At issue here is not so much age or unionization but two radically different strategies for managing a company's or a factory's work force, two incompatible views of what managers can reasonably expect of workers and of the kind of partnership they can share with them. For simplicity, I will speak of these profound differences as reflecting the choice between a strategy based on imposing *control* and a strategy based on eliciting *commitment.*

The 'control' strategy

The traditional – or control-oriented – approach to work-force management took shape during the early part of this century in response to the division of work into small, fixed jobs for which individuals could be held accountable. The actual definition of jobs, as of acceptable standards of performance, rested on "lowest common denominator" assumptions about workers' skill and motivation. To monitor and control effort of this assumed caliber, management organized its own responsibilities into a hierarchy of specialized roles buttressed by a top-down allocation of authority and by status symbols attached to positions in the hierarchy.

For workers, compensation followed the rubric of "a fair day's pay for a fair day's work" because precise evaluations were possible when individual job requirements were so carefully prescribed. Most managers had little doubt that labor was best thought of as a variable cost, although some exceptional companies guaranteed job security to head off unionization attempts.

In the traditional approach, there was generally little policy definition with regard to employee voice unless the work force was unionized, in which case damage control strategies predominated. With no union, management relied on an open-door policy, attitude surveys, and similar devices to learn about employees' concerns. If the work force was unionized, then management bargained terms of employment and established an appeal mechanism. These activities fell to labor relations specialists, who operated independently from line management and whose very existence assumed the inevitability and even the appropriateness of an adversarial relationship between workers and managers. Indeed, to those who saw management's exclusive obligation to be to a company's shareowners and the ownership of property to be the ultimate source of both obligation and prerogative, the claims of employees were constraints, nothing more.

At the heart of this traditional model is the wish to establish order, exercise control, and achieve efficiency in the application of the work force. Although it has distant antecedents in the bureaucracies of both church and military, the model's real father is Frederick W. Taylor, the turn-of-the-century "father of scientific management," whose views about the proper organization of work have long influenced management practice as well as the reactive policies of the U.S. labor movement.

Recently, however, changing expectations among workers have prompted a growing disillusionment with the apparatus of control. At the same time, of course, an intensified challenge from abroad has made the competitive obsolescence of this strategy clear. A model that assumes low employee commitment and that is designed to produce reliable if not outstanding performance simply cannot match the standards of excellence set by world-class competitors. Especially in a high-wage country like the United States, market success depends on a superior level of performance, a level that, in turn, requires the deep commitment, not merely the obedience – if you could obtain it – of workers. And as painful experience shows, this commitment cannot flourish in a workplace dominated by the familiar model of control.

The 'commitment' strategy

Since the early 1970s, companies have experimented at the plant level with a radically different work-force strategy. The more visible pioneers – among them, General Foods at Topeka, Kansas; General Motors at Brookhaven, Mississippi; Cummins Engine at Jamestown, New York; and Procter & Gamble at Lima, Ohio – have begun to show how great and productive the contribution of a truly committed work force can be. For a time, all new plants of this sort were nonunion, but by 1980 the success of efforts undertaken jointly with unions – GM's cooperation with the UAW at the Cadillac plant in Livonia, Michigan, for example – was impressive enough to encourage managers of both new and existing facilities to rethink their approach to the work force.

Stimulated in part by the dramatic turnaround at GM's Tarrytown assembly plant in the mid-1970s, local managers and union officials are increasingly talking about common interests, working to develop mutual trust, and agreeing to sponsor quality-of-work-life (QWL) or employee involvement (EI) activities. Although most of these ventures have been initiated at the local level, major exceptions include the joint effort between the Communication Workers of America and AT&T to promote QWL throughout the Bell System and the UAW-Ford EI program centrally directed by Donald Ephlin of the UAW and Peter Pestillo of Ford. In the nonunion sphere, the spirit of these new initiatives is evident in the decision by workers of Delta Airlines to show their commitment to the company by collecting money to buy a new plane.

More recently, a growing number of manufacturing companies has begun to remove levels of plant hierarchy, increase managers' spans of control, integrate quality and production activities at lower organizational levels, combine production and maintenance operations, and open up new career possibilities for workers. Some corporations have even begun to chart organizational renewal for the entire company. Cummins Engine, for example, has ambitiously committed itself to inform employees about the business, to encourage participation by everyone, and to create jobs that involve greater responsibility and more flexibility.

In this new commitment-based approach to the work force, jobs are designed to be broader than before, to combine planning and implementation, and to include efforts to upgrade operations, not just maintain them. Individual responsibilities are expected to change as conditions change, and teams, not individuals, often are the organizational units accountable for performance. With management hierarchies relatively flat and differences in status minimized, control and lateral coordination depend on shared goals, and expertise rather than formal position determines influence.

People Express, to cite one example, started up with its management hierarchy limited to three levels, organized its work force into three- or four-person groups, and created positions with exceptionally broad scope. Every full-time employee is a "manager": flight managers are pilots who also perform dispatching and safety checks; maintenance managers are technicians with other staff responsibilities; customer service managers take care of ticketing, security clearance, passenger boarding, and in-flight service. Everyone, including the officers, is expected to rotate among functions to boost all workers' understanding of the business and to promote personal development.

Under the commitment strategy, performance expectations are high and serve not to define minimum standards but to provide "stretch objectives," emphasize continuous improvement, and reflect the requirements of the marketplace. Accordingly, compensation policies reflect less the old formulas of job evaluation than the heightened importance of group achievement, the expanded scope of individual contribution, and the growing concern for such questions of "equity" as gain sharing, stock ownership, and profit sharing. This principle of economic sharing is not new. It has long played a role in Dana Corporation, which has many unionized plants, and is a fundamental part of the strategy of People Express, which has no union. Today, Ford sees it as an important part of the company's transition to a commitment strategy.

Equally important to the commitment strategy is the challenge of giving employees some assurance of security, perhaps by offering them priority in training and retraining as old jobs are eliminated and new ones created. Guaranteeing employees access to due process and providing them the means to be heard on such issues as production methods, problem solving, and human resource policies and practices is also a challenge. In unionized settings, the additional tasks include making relations less adversarial, broadening the agenda for joint problem solving and planning, and facilitating employee consultation.

Underlying all these policies is a management philosophy, often embodied in a published statement, that acknowledges the legitimate claims of a company's multiple stakeholders—owners, employees, customers, and the public. At the center of this philosophy is a belief that eliciting employee commitment will lead to enhanced performance. The evidence shows this belief to be well-grounded. In the absence of genuine commitment, however, new management policies designed for a committed work force may well leave a company distinctly more vulnerable than would older policies based on the control approach. The advantages—and risks—are considerable.

The costs of commitment

Because the potential leverage of a commitment-oriented strategy on performance is so great, the natural temptation is to assume the universal applicability of that strategy. Some environments, however, especially those requiring intricate teamwork, problem solving, organizational learning, and self-monitoring, are better suited than others to the commitment model. Indeed, the pioneers of the deep commitment strategy—a fertilizer plant in Norway, a refinery in the United Kingdom, a paper mill in Pennsylvania, a pet-food processing plant in Kansas—were all based on continuous process technologies and were all capital and raw material intensive. All provided high economic leverage to improvements in workers' skills and attitudes, and all could offer considerable job challenge.

Is the converse true? Is the control strategy appropriate whenever—as with convicts breaking rocks with sledgehammers in a prison yard—work can be completely prescribed, remains static, and calls for individual, not group, effort? In practice, managers have long answered yes. Mass production, epitomized by the assembly line, has for years been thought suitable for old-fashioned control.

But not any longer. Many mass producers, not least the automakers, have recently been trying to reconceive the structure of work and to give employees a significant role in solving problems and improving methods. Why? For many reasons, including to boost in-plant quality, lower warranty costs, cut waste, raise machine utilization and total capacity with the same plant and equipment, reduce operating and support personnel, reduce turnover and absenteeism, and speed up implementation of change. In addition, some managers place direct value on the fact that the commitment policies promote the development of human skills and individual self-esteem.

The benefits, economic and human, of worker commitment extend not only to continuous-process industries but to traditional manufacturing industries as well. What, though, are the costs? To achieve these gains, managers have had to invest extra effort, develop new skills and relationships, cope with higher levels of ambiguity and uncertainty, and experience the pain and discomfort associated with changing habits and attitudes. Some of their skills have become obsolete, and some of their careers have been casualties of change. Union officials, too, have had to face the dislocation and discomfort that inevitably follow any upheaval in attitudes and skills. For their part, workers have inherited more responsibility and, along with it, greater uncertainty and a more open-ended possibility of failure.

Part of the difficulty in assessing these costs is the fact that so many of the following problems inherent to the commitment strategy remain to be solved.

Employment assurances

As managers in heavy industry confront economic realities that make such assurances less feasible and as their counterparts in fiercely competitive high-technology areas are forced to rethink early guarantees of employment security, pointed questions await.

Will managers give lifetime assurances to the few, those who reach, say, 15 years' seniority, or will they adopt a general no-layoff policy? Will they demonstrate by policies and practices that employment security, though by no means absolute, is a higher priority item than it was under the control approach? Will they accept greater responsibility for outplacement?

Compensation

In one sense, the more productive employees under the commitment approach deserve to receive better pay for their better efforts, but how can managers balance this claim on resources with the harsh reality that domestic pay rates have risen to levels that render many of our industries uncompetitive

Exhibit   Work-force strategies

	Control	Transitional	Commitment
Job design principles	Individual attention limited to performing individual job.	Scope of individual responsibility extended to upgrading system performance, via participative problem-solving groups in QWL, EI, and quality circle programs.	Individual responsibility extended to upgrading system performance.
	Job design deskills and fragments work and separates doing and thinking.	No change in traditional job design or accountability.	Job design enhances content of work, emphasizes whole task, and combines doing and thinking.
	Accountability focused on individual.		Frequent use of teams as basic accountable unit.
	Fixed job definition.		Flexible definition of duties, contingent on changing conditions.
Performance expectations	Measured standards define minimum performance. Stability seen as desirable.		Emphasis placed on higher, "stretch objectives," which tend to be dynamic and oriented to the marketplace.
Management organization: structure, systems, and style	Structure tends to be layered, with top-down controls.	No basic changes in approaches to structure, control, or authority.	Flat organization structure with mutual influence systems.
	Coordination and control rely on rules and procedures.		Coordination and control based more on shared goals, values, and traditions.
	More emphasis on prerogatives and positional authority.		Management emphasis on problem solving and relevant information and expertise.
	Status symbols distributed to reinforce hierarchy.	A few visible symbols change.	Minimum status differentials to de-emphasize inherent hierarchy.
Compensation policies	Variable pay where feasible to provide individual incentive.	Typically no basic changes in compensation concepts.	Variable rewards to create equity and to reinforce group achievements: gain sharing, profit sharing.
	Individual pay geared to job evaluation.		Individual pay linked to skills and mastery.
	In downturn, cuts concentrated on hourly payroll.	Equality of sacrifice among employee groups.	Equality of sacrifice.
Employment assurances	Employees regarded as variable costs.	Assurances that participation will not result in loss of job.	Assurances that participation will not result in loss of job.
		Extra effort to avoid layoffs.	High commitment to avoid or assist in reemployment.
			Priority for training and retaining existing work force.
Employee voice policies	Employee input allowed on relatively narrow agenda. Attendant risks emphasized. Methods include open-door policy, attitude surveys, grievance procedures, and collective bargaining in some organizations.	Addition of limited, ad hoc consultation mechanisms. No change in corporate governance.	Employee participation encouraged on wide range of issues. Attendant benefits emphasized. New concepts of corporate governance.
	Business information distributed on strictly defined "need to know" basis.	Additional sharing of information.	Business data shared widely.
Labor-management relations	Adversarial labor relations; emphasis on interest conflict.	Thawing of adversarial attitudes; joint sponsorship of QWL or EI; emphasis on common fate.	Mutuality in labor relations; joint planning and problem solving on expanded agenda.
			Unions, management, and workers redefine their respective roles.

internationally? Already, in such industries as trucking and airlines, new domestic competitors have placed companies that maintain prevailing wage rates at a significant disadvantage. Experience shows, however, that wage freezes and concession bargaining create obstacles to commitment, and new approaches to compensation are difficult to develop at a time when management cannot raise the overall level of pay.

Which approach is really suitable to the commitment model is unclear. Traditional job classifications place limits on the discretion of supervisors and encourage workers' sense of job ownership. Can pay systems based on employees' skill levels, which have long been used in engineering and skilled crafts, prove widely effective? Can these systems make up in greater mastery, positive motivation, and workforce flexibility what they give away in higher average wages?

In capital-intensive businesses, where total payroll accounts for a small percentage of costs, economics favor the move toward pay progression based on deeper and broader mastery. Still, conceptual problems remain with measuring skills, achieving consistency in pay decisions, allocating opportunities for learning new skills, trading off breadth and flexibility against depth, and handling the effects of "topping out" in a system that rewards and encourages personal growth.

There are also practical difficulties. Existing plants cannot, for example, convert to a skill-based structure overnight because of the vested interests of employees in the higher classifications. Similarly, formal profit- or gain-sharing plans like the Scanlon Plan (which shares gains in productivity as measured by improvements in the ratio of payroll to the sales value of production) cannot always operate. At the plant level, formulas that are responsive to what employees can influence, that are not unduly influenced by factors beyond their control, and that are readily understood, are not easy to devise. Small stand-alone businesses with a mature technology and stable markets tend to find the task least troublesome, but they are not the only ones trying to implement the commitment approach.

Yet another problem, very much at issue in the Hyatt-Clark bearing plant, which employees purchased from General Motors in 1981, is the relationship between compensation decisions affecting salaried managers and professionals, on the one hand, and hourly workers, on the other. When they formed the company, workers took a 25% pay cut to make their bearings competitive but the managers maintained and, in certain instances increased, their own salaries in order to help the company attract and retain critical talent. A manager's ability to elicit and preserve commitment, however, is sensitive to issues of equity, as became evident once again when GM and Ford announced huge executive bonuses in the spring of 1984 while keeping hourly wages capped.

Technology

Computer-based technology can reinforce the control model or facilitate movement to the commitment model. Applications can narrow the scope of jobs or broaden them, emphasize the individual nature of tasks or promote the work of groups, centralize or decentralize the making of decisions, and create performance measures that emphasize learning or hierarchical control.

To date, the effects of this technology on control and commitment have been largely unintentional and unexpected. Even in organizations otherwise pursuing a commitment strategy, managers have rarely appreciated that the side effects of technology are not somehow "given" in the nature of things or that they can be actively managed. In fact, computer-based technology may be the least deterministic, most flexible technology to enter the workplace since the industrial revolution. As it becomes less hardware-dependent and more software-intensive and as the cost of computer power declines, the variety of ways to meet business requirements expands, each with a different set of human implications. Management has yet to identify the potential role of technology policy in the commitment strategy, and it has yet to invent concepts and methods to realize that potential.

Supervisors

The commitment model requires first-line supervisors to facilitate rather than direct the work force, to impart rather than merely practice their technical and administrative expertise, and to help workers develop the ability to manage themselves. In practice, supervisors are to delegate away most of their traditional functions—often without having received adequate training and support for their new team-building tasks or having their own needs for voice, dignity, and fulfillment recognized.

These dilemmas are even visible in the new titles many supervisors carry—"team advisers" or "team consultants," for example—most of which imply that supervisors are not in the chain of command, although they are expected to be directive if necessary and assume functions delegated to the work force if they are not being performed. Part of the confusion here is the failure to distinguish the behavioral style required of supervisors from the basic responsibilities assigned them. Their ideal style may be advisory, but their responsibilities are to achieve certain human and economic outcomes. With experience, however, as first-line managers become more comfortable with the notion of delegating what subordinates are ready and able to perform, the problem will diminish.

Other difficulties are less tractable. The new breed of supervisors must have a level of interpersonal skill and conceptual ability often lacking in the present supervisory work force. Some companies have tried to address this lack by using the position as an entry point to management for college graduates. This approach may succeed where the work force has already acquired the necessary technical expertise, but it blocks a route of advancement for workers and sharpens the dividing line between management and other employees. Moreover, unless the company intends to open up higher level positions for these college-educated supervisors, they may well grow impatient with the shift work of first-line supervision.

Even when new supervisory roles are filled—and filled successfully—from the ranks, dilemmas remain. With teams developed and functions delegated, to what new challenges do they turn to utilize fully their own capabilities? Do those capabilities match the demands of the other managerial work they might take on? If fewer and fewer supervisors are required as their individual span of control extends to a second and a third work team, what promotional opportunities exist for the rest? Where do they go?

Union-management relations

Some companies, as they move from control to commitment, seek to decertify their unions and, at the same time, strengthen their employees' bond to the company. Others—like GM, Ford, Jones & Laughlin, and AT&T—pursue cooperation with their unions, believing that they need their active support. Management's interest in cooperation intensified in the late 1970s, as improved work-force effectiveness could not by itself close the competitive gap in many industries and wage concessions became necessary. Based on their own analysis of competitive conditions, unions sometimes agreed to these concessions but expanded their influence over matters previously subject to management control.

These developments open up new questions. Where companies are trying to preserve the nonunion status of some plants and yet promote collaborative union relations in others, will unions increasingly force the company to choose? After General Motors saw the potential of its joint QWL program with the UAW, it signed a neutrality clause (in 1976) and then an understanding about automatic recognition in new plants (in 1979). If forced to choose, what will other managements do? Further, where union and management have collaborated in promoting QWL, how can the union prevent management from using the program to appeal directly to the workers about issues, such as wage concessions, that are subject to collective bargaining?

And if, in the spirit of mutuality, both sides agree to expand their joint agenda, what new risks will they face? Do union officials have the expertise to deal effectively with new agenda items like investment, pricing, and technology? To support QWL activities, they already have had to expand their skills and commit substantial resources at a time when shrinking employment has reduced their membership and thus their finances.

The transitional stage

Although some organizations have adopted a comprehensive version of the commitment approach, most initially take on a more limited set of changes, which I refer to as a "transitional" stage or approach. The challenge here is to modify expectations, to make credible the leaders' stated intentions for further movement, and to support the initial changes in behavior. These transitional efforts can achieve a temporary equilibrium, provided they are viewed as part of a movement toward a comprehensive commitment strategy.

The cornerstone of the transitional stage is the voluntary participation of employees in problem-solving groups like quality circles. In unionized organizations, union-management dialogue leading to a jointly sponsored program is a condition for this type of employee involvement, which must then be supported by additional training and communication and by a shift in management style. Managers must also seek ways to consult employees about changes that affect them and to assure them that management will make every effort to avoid, defer, or minimize layoffs from higher productivity. When volume-related layoffs or concessions on pay are unavoidable, the principle of "equality of sacrifice" must apply to all employee groups, not just the hourly work force.

As a rule, during the early stages of transformation, few immediate changes can occur in the basic design of jobs, the compensation system, or the management system itself. It is easy, of course, to attempt to change too much too soon. A more common error, especially in established organizations, is to make only "token" changes that never reach a critical mass. All too often managers try a succession of technique-oriented changes one by one: job enrichment, sensitivity training, management by objectives, group brainstorming, quality circles, and so on. Whatever the benefits of these techniques, their value to the organization will rapidly decay if the management philosophy—and practice—does not shift accordingly.

A different type of error—"overreaching"—may occur in newly established organizations based on commitment principles. In one new plant, managers allowed too much peer influence in pay decisions; in another, they underplayed the role of first-line supervisors as a link in the chain of command; in a third, they overemphasized learning of new skills and flexibility at the expense of mastery in critical operations. These design errors by themselves are not fatal, but the organization must be able to make mid-course corrections.

Rate of transformation

How rapidly is the transformation in work-force strategy, summarized in the *Exhibit,* occurring? Hard data are difficult to come by, but certain trends are clear. In 1970, only a few plants in the United States were systematically revising their approach to the work force. By 1975, hundreds of plants were involved. Today, I estimate that at least a thousand plants are in the process of making a comprehensive change and that many times that number are somewhere in the transitional stage.

In the early 1970s, plant managers tended to sponsor what efforts there were. Today, company presidents are formulating the plans. Not long ago, the initiatives were experimental; now they are policy. Early change focused on the blue-collar work force and on those clerical operations that most closely resemble the factory. Although clerical change has lagged somewhat—because the control model has not produced such overt employee disaffection, and because management has been slow to recognize the importance of quality and productivity improvement—there are signs of a quickened pace of change in clerical operations.

Only a small fraction of U.S. workplaces today can boast of a comprehensive commitment strategy, but the rate of transformation continues to accelerate, and the move toward commitment via some explicit transitional stage extends to a still larger number of plants and offices. This transformation may be fueled by economic necessity, but other factors are shaping and pacing it—individual leadership in management and labor, philosophical choices, organizational competence in managing change, and cumulative learning from change itself.

Suggested readings

Irving Bluestone,
"Labor's Stake in Improving the Quality of Working Life,"
The Quality of Working Life and the 1980s,
ed. Harvey Kolodny and Hans van Beinum
(New York: Praeger, 1983).

Robert H. Guest,
"Quality of Work Life—Learning from Tarrytown,"
HBR July-August 1979, p. 76.

Janice A. Klein,
"Why Supervisors Resist Employee Involvement,"
HBR September-October 1984, p. 87.

John F. Runcie,
" 'By Days I Make the Cars',"
HBR May-June 1980, p. 106.

W. Earl Sasser and Frank S. Leonard,
"Let First-Level Supervisors Do Their Job,"
HBR March-April 1980, p. 113.

Leonard A. Schlesinger and Janice A. Klein,
"The First-Line Supervisor: Past, Present and Future,"
Handbook of Organizational Behavior,
ed. Jay W. Lorsch
(Englewood Cliffs, N.J.: Prentice-Hall, 1983).

Richard E. Walton,
"Work Innovations in the United States,"
HBR July-August 1979, p. 88;
"Improving the Quality of Work Life,"
HBR May-June 1974, p. 12;
"How to Counter Alienation in the Plant,"
HBR November-December 1972, p. 70.
Richard E. Walton and Wendy Vittori,
"New Information Technology:
Organizational Problem or Opportunity?"
Office: Technology and People,
No. 1, 1983, p. 249.
Richard E. Walton and Leonard A. Schlesinger,
"Do Supervisors Thrive in Participative Work Systems?"
Organizational Dynamics,
Winter 1979, p. 25.

Reprint 85219

People policies for the new machines

Richard E. Walton and Gerald I. Susman

Human resource policies and practices once associated only with progressive management philosophies now look desirable from a technological perspective as well. Part of the reason is that advanced manufacturing technology (AMT) makes human skills and workers' commitment more important than ever. So, many leading-edge manufacturers are searching for ways to enhance their workers' capabilities and improve labor relations, even as they look to the new technology to cut labor costs overall.

Look at what happens when AMT is introduced into a workplace. In plant after plant we see:

Closer interdependence among activities.

Different skill requirements – usually higher average skill levels.

More immediate – and more costly – consequences of any malfunction.

Output more sensitive to variations in human skills, knowledge, and attitudes, and to mental effort rather than physical effort.

More dynamism, that is, continual change and development.

Higher capital investment per employee and fewer employees responsible for a particular product, part, or process.

Most of these characteristics appear when any computer-based technology is brought into a plant, of course. But in the early stages of stand-alone automation (when a company installs numerical control machines, say, or automated testing machinery) management still has a choice between raising or lowering skill requirements and coupling or decoupling activities. As pieces of automation and information technology are integrated, however, interdependence becomes a fact of life and jobs designed with higher skill requirements become essential. Just-in-time inventory policies and "make it right the first time" approaches reinforce these trends.

These conclusions reflect what we saw in the field as members of a National Research Council committee.[1] During 1985, we visited 16 plants and reviewed practices in 8 others that are pioneering in AMT.[2] (*Exhibit I* describes the sites.) Out of the human resource practices we observed, we developed a model to help executives – and labor leaders, where they are involved – think about AMT's implications and develop strategies to make the new machines effective.

HR strategies

By now, almost everyone is familiar with AMT in some form. Briefly, the term refers to sev-

Mr. Walton, the Jesse Isidor Straus Professor of Business Administration at the Harvard Business School, is a pioneer authority on work-force management issues. His HBR article, "How to Counter Alienation in the Plant" (November-December 1972), was one of the first analyses of participative management. He chaired the National Research Council committee whose work is reported here.

Mr. Susman is professor of organizational behavior at the College of Business Administration at the Pennsylvania State University and director of its Center for the Management of Technological and Organizational Change. He was study director of the National Research Council committee.

eral types of technology, including computer-aided manufacturing, computer-aided design and engineering, manufacturing resource planning, and computer-aided process planning.

Until recently, most companies took a piece-by-piece approach to this new technology and thereby created islands of automation. Now, however, the new machines are beginning to speak through local-area networks. As they do, it becomes essential to have:

A highly skilled, flexible, coordinated, and committed work force.

Lean, flat, flexible, and innovative management.

The ability to retain developed talent.

A strong partnership between management and labor unions.

Looking at the practices that companies were adopting to fulfill these needs, we saw patterns in how they approached job design, work-force and management organization, compensation, appraisal, selection, and training.

Job design. Even without the stimulus of new technology, many companies have begun replacing rigid, narrow jobs with broader ones to motivate workers and enhance operational flexibility. With the introduction of AMT, managers see even greater potential in such changes. Broadening operating jobs, for example, to include functions that support staff has been handling saves overhead, and combining interrelated operating tasks reduces waiting time. Both changes also promote a sense of ownership among workers and enhance operational flexibility.

Multiskilled operators in an automated appliance line we reviewed, for example, had responsibility for materials handling, setup, troubleshooting, and off-line repair of defective units—functions once performed by different groups, each respecting jurisdictional lines that the union vigorously enforced. In a computer products plant, operators had similar duties but in addition were expected to gradually take on more maintenance responsibilities. Freed-up maintenance technicians in turn took on more engineering functions. When companies couldn't create jobs as challenging as these, they rotated lower skilled tasks and gave workers more autonomy.

These trends mesh with AMT for several reasons. First, the more integrated the AMT, the more alert and ready to act workers must be. AMT automates many repetitive activities, and those that remain, like loading a machine, are necessary less often, so it would be easy for workers to become inattentive. Yet it's even more vital that they know how to adjust equipment and when to ask for help. Knowing exactly what action to take calls for communication and diagnostic problem-solving skills among workers, maintenance supervisors, and support personnel.

Because the technology requires workers to be alert and take initiatives rather than just perform physical work, it is crucial that operators be motivated internally. In technologies that involve repetitive, short-cycle activities, close supervision can compensate partly for lack of motivation. But supervision cannot replace individual responsibility in the complex environment AMT creates.

Consider, for example, the high cost and immediate consequences of errors. Since the time between detecting an error and acting on it should be as short as possible, combining these responsibilities is advisable. And, in fact, companies are finding more pluses than minuses in giving workers responsibility for monitoring new technology as well as operating it.

The new technology is also conducive to fewer job classifications: an axle plant, for example, has reduced hourly job classifications to just three—two skilled and one unskilled; a nonunion electronics plant has gone from seven to one in one department. Such reductions can occur because the activities involved in working with AMT—like monitoring and maintenance—are largely the same. So there's less need to differentiate among similar jobs throughout the factory. The tighter interdependence of the tasks, of course, also makes flexibility in assignments extremely advantageous.

A corollary of the trend toward fewer, broader job classifications is the upgrading of workers' skills. At one plant where multiskilled operators took on maintenance functions and maintenance technicians took on engineering tasks, the diffusion of other forms of automation throughout the facilities affected many more hourly workers as well. Some manual assemblers progressed to more complicated assembly units, while others graduated to testing jobs, which were also becoming more complicated. Workers reported that because of these changes, their jobs had become more meaningful and they themselves more marketable.

Work-team structure. AMT both increases the incentive for managers to install formal

---

1 For a full report on this research, see Committee on the Effective Implementation of Advanced Manufacturing Technology, *Human Resource Practices for Implementing Advanced Manufacturing Technology* (Washington, D.C.: National Academy Press, 1986). The committee was comprised of four business executives, two trade union officials, and three university professors.

2 The committee reviewed plants of the following companies: Consolidated Diesel Company, Cummins Engine Company Inc., FMC Corporation, Ford Motor Company, C.L. Frost & Sons, Inc., General Electric Company, General Motors Company, Grumman Corporation, Honeywell Inc., International Business Machines Corporation, Ingersoll Milling Machine Company, McDonnell Douglas Corporation, and Rockwell International.

team structures and makes them easier to implement, for several reasons:

    1   Interdependence makes it less feasible to hold people accountable for a single bounded task; AMT often calls for smaller organizational units responsible for making an entire product or part, and teams recognize shared responsibility for performance.

    2   Teams help create a sense of responsibility among lower level employees, a critical need of AMT.

    3   Data for diagnosing complex systems can be shared more easily within and across teams.

    4   A well-run work group is a powerful mechanism for securing commitment to demanding goals—a vital factor because of the big capital investment involved.

The companies we visited were relying more on team processes, but they varied in the formality and autonomy of their teams. These differences partly reflected the way work groups had operated before the introduction of AMT. Two facilities, for example, had committed themselves to a team structure before the start-up of AMT, and the teams responsible for the new technology just reinforced an established pattern. The manager of one of these, an engine plant, had divided the shop floor into about 20 teams of "technicians" with 20 to 30 workers on each team. The teams had different styles of self-management. Almost all had informal leaders, and some rotated the post among members. Some teams met daily, some weekly to discuss problems. All had analyzed and divided their work into modules that workers were expected to master progressively over several years.

Other companies had committed themselves to teams when they implemented AMT. The axle plant, for example, introduced "shift operation groups," each made up of 20 hourly employees—12 system attendants, 4 electricians, and 4 machine repairmen—supported by a maintenance engineer and a quality engineer on each shift, plus a factory control administrator. Subteams in each of four zones are responsible for four or five different machine functions. In hiring, management emphasizes the development of team processes and looks for people who are capable of managing themselves. Other facilities, like the appliance and the computer products plants, use a less structured approach. In these companies, executives have promoted teamwork among the multiskilled operators, whom they see as sharing responsibility for an automated line. But they have not created formal teams like the axle plant's.

Not all companies, however, opt for teams. In an office equipment plant undergoing a $350 million renovation, management delegates more authority to operators, but only for their assigned tasks. The workers, called "owner-operators," monitor equipment and supplies, make corrective adjustments, and perform minor maintenance on their machines. But they do not coordinate these tasks, as they would under a team system. Whether this will change with time remains to be seen. When we visited the plant, the renovation was only 60% completed.

Compensation and appraisal. Changes in job design and work structure affected how employees are appraised and compensated at the plants. Policies concerning pay levels, salary versus hourly status, and bases for pay progression all needed to be reviewed. The variety of methods being tried, however, suggests that no consensus has emerged on the best ways to evaluate and reward workers. In almost every case we studied, workers' pay stayed the same or rose as a result of AMT. Sometimes pay increased because jobs were broader and multiskilled. In other cases, individual pay didn't rise, but average plant pay did as the least skilled and lowest paying jobs were eliminated. Management couldn't forecast whether total take-home pay would be higher once a company's AMT was up and running. Presumably overtime would decrease after the debugging period, when plants would be running 16 to 24 hours a day and multiskilled workers were available on all shifts.

Of the 16 plants we visited, 5 have put workers on weekly salary, at least in part in an effort to mute status differences between management and labor. Salaries are more justifiable than hourly pay, anyway, as labor becomes a fixed rather than a variable cost. Operating a highly automated plant takes the same number of workers whether or not the plant is running at capacity.

Another tack, taken at several sites, is to replace standard job classification systems with pay-for-knowledge systems, which adjust workers' wages according to their mastery of "work modules," or clusters of tasks. For example, the engine plant, whose work teams we described earlier, has 50 modules that employees are expected to learn over a 9- to 15-month period. Some of the modules are in the machining or assembly lines; others are in the tooling areas and material stores. Workers decide, with advice, what modules they will learn, and they develop plans for getting the training and experience they will need. The plant's long-term plan is to organize a much larger set of modules into levels of increasing pay and responsibility. The whole set will take several years to master.

The number of work modules a worker can perform is an index of the person's capacity to contribute. Certifying a worker's mastery of any particular module is often a subjective judgment, however, as is determining whether employees are applying their mastery diligently to detect machine malfunctions, perform as problem solvers, and contribute as team

Exhibit I Plants visited by the research committee

	Product	Number of employees	Union status	Location	Year implementation began	Technology installed
Existing sites	Electronic components	2,000	Nonunion	Southeast	1984	R, MH, T, Laser engraving
	Electronic components	3,300	Nonunion	Southwest	1985	MRP II (10 modules)
	Aircraft	18,200	Nonunion	Northeast	1985	R, S
	Aircraft	24,000	Union	Midwest	1985	S
	Office equipment	6,000	Nonunion	Southeast	1983	R, MH, AGV, AS/RS
	Materials handling equipment	115	Nonunion	Midwest	1984	CNC, R, FMS
	Engines	4,385	Union	Midwest	1985	FMS
	Automobile components	54	Nonunion	Southwest	1985	R, T
	Engines	6,500	Union	Midwest	1982	FMS
	Machine tools	1,500	Nonunion	Midwest	1984	FMS
Greenfield sites	Engines	400	Nonunion	Southeast	1981	CNC, R, MH, T
	Military vehicle components	370	Nonunion	Southeast	1982	CNC, R, AGV
	Automobile components	1,460	Union	Canada	1981	R, T
	Automobile assembly	6,700	Union	Midwest	1982	R, MH, AGV
	Automobile assembly	2,400	Union	Midwest	1982	R, MH
	Automobile components	48*	Union	Midwest	1983	FMS, DNC, MH

*Surrounding facility employs 10,000.

Key to technology
R = robots
MH = automated materials handling
T = computer-aided testing
MRP II = manufacturing resource planning
S = specialized fabrication equipment
AGV = automated guided vehicle
AS/RS = automated storage and retrieval system
CNC = computerized numerical control
FMS = flexible manufacturing systems
DNC = direct numerical control

---

members. Whether made by supervisors or by a worker's fellow team members, these decisions are hard calls.

Piece rates and other pay-for-performance systems that focus on an individual's output are less appropriate with the new technology. Aspects of performance that can be measured objectively, like throughput, quality, waste, and downtime, seldom can be attributed to one person; they reflect the interdependent contributions of operators, supervisors, and maintenance and other support personnel. We did not, however, see any group bonuses, perhaps in part because few systems had reached the steady-state operating mode that would permit meaningful standards to be set.

Emphasizing team accomplishments does not eliminate the need for assessing individual performance, but it does call for new methods. In plants that make merit adjustments within a pay range, for example, managers have had to change their appraisal system. In the computer products plant, executives reported that they continued to assess performance in terms of individual output in the manual assembly lines. But in the automated line they had to assess individual performance in more qualitative terms—like contributions of ideas and efforts to the group's work.

The design and administration of compensation and appraisal systems may become more complex with AMT, but we cannot say that they become more important. If anything, employee motivation is less dependent on extrinsic rewards and more responsive to other changes, like broader jobs, training and mastery of new skills, and well-managed work teams.

Management organization. AMT demands coordination at every level of a factory's organization, so it's not surprising that many senior managers are intensely interested in developing new organizational forms and management styles. Most of the plants we visited had reduced the number of layers and had integrated support functions closer to the factory floor. They had upgraded supervisors and assigned them functions previously performed by second-level managers. For example, an engine plant with only four management levels has given its support services—like tooling and material stores—to first-level area managers. Similarly, an electronics equipment plant has put first-level managers in charge of $10 million "minibusinesses," to which information services, quality control, and packaging were reassigned.

This tendency to push operating decisions downward involves complicated dynamics. As the manager of an appliance factory pointed out, the plant's information system can alert all management levels simultaneously to problems that before might have languished at lower levels. And in the tightly coupled production system (with four or five hours of inventory), problems that once might have taken weeks to surface now pop up quickly. "So in one way, I'm more involved in process details," said the plant manager, "because they bubble up faster and have more serious consequences. On the other hand, I delegate more—because those close to the process have to think and act fast."

Several plants have developed mechanisms for consultative decision making. The superintendent of the axle plant, for example, heads a plant operations committee consisting of representatives from finance, manufacturing, engineering, and electronic systems, as well as shift workers and union people. Shift operations groups report to this committee, which shares information with them. Committee members make decisions after consultation with one another, and they seek consensus.

Managers slated to direct AMT were often involved in planning its implementation. They were selected well before the new technology became operational and were assigned full- or part-time to the implementation team. Often company leaders were careful to select managers whose values agreed with the desired culture and who could promote teamwork, participative problem solving, and open communication.

Companies contemplating AMT need to give even more thought to the selection and development of manufacturing managers. Future managers will need a broader range of competence than their predecessors. They will have to know the technology and be able to grasp (practically and conceptually) the technical, human, and business aspects of production. They must also be able to anticipate and orchestrate change in the organization.

Selection and training. In virtually every plant we visited, management had tried to revise and upgrade the way it selected and trained workers for AMT. In general, the ability to learn was becoming more important than experience. Also, some assessment methods that had only been used with managers (like group problem-solving simulations) were being applied to production workers.

The appliance plant's procedures were typical of facilities where management introduced only modest changes. The managers classified the new, multiskilled operator above other jobs—in part to minimize bumping during layoffs—but they instituted no new selection procedures. Accordingly, they ran into problems when the new pay rate for this job attracted 50 bids for the first 6 positions—many from applicants who lacked the basic verbal and quantitative skills to absorb the training. The labor contract mandated training for the senior employees who bid on the job, however, so management's only screening option was to spell out the job's multiple duties and encourage self-selection. Although about half the applicants withdrew, the managers realized they had to negotiate a change in the selection process so that the most proficient operators would have a chance at the training.

We observed more innovative selection processes in several other unionized plants. At the axle plant, for example, applicants for skilled jobs completed an eight-hour assessment of their technical and interpersonal skills, conducted by a local community college. They were given a four- to six-hour skill-level inventory, which included simulated problem-solving exercises, and then attended a family night with their spouses to discuss the program. The 45 applicants who remained from an initial group of 100 were then ranked by seniority. Some of them declined the new jobs; 16 were eventually placed. Many dropped out because working in the new plant involved shift work or demanded higher performance standards than they were prepared to accept. Others declined because they felt unqualified or had only a few years to go before retirement and didn't want to waste the company's investment.

Buying automation buys more than technology.

A unionized diesel engine plant devised a multistep process in which the 250 initial applicants were divided into small groups and given a four-hour briefing on the technology and the new job's duties and expectations. Those who persisted were interviewed by a committee of two manufacturing supervisors and two union representatives. The union reps went out of their way to warn applicants how different the new operation would be and cautioned them to reflect on their interests and aptitudes. Taking the interview results into account, as well as attendance records, seniority, experience, and any evaluation records, the same committee made the final selection. From this and similar efforts, we conclude that managements and unions can devise ways to consider criteria other than seniority without losing workers' confidence in the fairness of the selection process.

Why should unions seek these innovations? Union officials, as much as their counterparts in management, often appreciated the importance of selecting people who would be able to perform well. They understood that the effectiveness of the new technology—and thus the plant's competitiveness—would depend on the operators. And they were concerned about wasting money training the wrong people. Moreover, when union leaders expressed these views, the workers tended to espouse them too.

Training practices associated with AMT included much larger lead times, joint sessions for workers and managers, programs designed to develop basic knowledge as well as specific skills, and a commitment to continuous training. The following examples are representative:

☐ The management of an auto assembly plant established a training center months before an automated factory was to become operational and taught its skilled workers to use the new equipment across their trade lines. The employees also received training in communication skills so that they could contribute to weekly problem-solving meetings. All these workers, who were transferring to the facility from other plants, had more than a year of training before completion of the plant.

☐ At a military vehicle components factory, all shop employees must attend a three-month pre-hire training program at a local technical institution to master machining principles and acquire hands-on experience with some of the technology. During the course, they are tested and management monitors their progress. Upon graduation they become eligible for the jobs as they become available.

☐ Workers in the axle plant underwent an extensive skills-assessment program and received technological training designed by faculty at a local community college.

☐ An engine plant sent its engineers and skilled workers to a vendor's school to be trained in maintaining programmable controllers. One executive commented, "A few years ago, we never would have spent money to send production people to courses."

AMT is changing constantly, making continuous training mandatory. One company calculated that the occupational "half-life" (the time in which one-half of a worker's knowledge and skills become obsolete) has declined from a range of 7 to 14 years to 3 to 5 years. As a result, this company and others we studied were developing the capacity to train their employees continuously. And even so, most of the managers also admitted that they had underestimated the funds and organizational resources needed for the training process.

Fortunately, however, companies aren't the only ones investing in training. We observed many workers training for AMT jobs after hours by enrolling in community colleges or local technical institutes.

Upgrading & downgrading

The policy choices we have described (particularly those related to job design, selection, and training) constitute a strategy to upgrade workers' knowledge and skills. Had management simply followed practice, the more demanding AMT tasks in most of the companies we reviewed probably would have been assigned to managers or other professionals. Whether they use the term explicitly or not, companies seem to be weighing benefits and risks and deciding in favor of upgrading. Downgrading, however, remains a live option in the minds of some managements, and the choice is still a judgment call.

Downgrading assumes that middle managers and support personnel will deal with all serious problems, either by taking action themselves or by writing software that solves them. Because workers perform only the simpler tasks, it is easier to instruct and monitor their performance, and it is easier to replace them. Moreover, because they are less skilled, workers can be paid less or at least no more than they were on their old jobs. Management in unionized settings may also reduce vulnerability to strikes by assigning most programming and monitoring functions to white-collar, nonunion workers.

Still, downgrading incurs costs and carries great risk. First, paying middle managers and support personnel in these settings costs more. Second, low-skilled workers are less likely to recognize a problem before it becomes serious, and their understanding of the technical system may not permit them to interpret warning cues correctly. Third, downgrading can short-circuit an important learning loop by cutting the links between those who recognize incipient problems and those who diagnose and solve them. Fourth, in unionized settings, assigning programming and monitoring functions to white-collar, nonunion workers can undermine labor-management relations if union members believe these functions should be assigned to them. Many of these risks increase as the AMT becomes broader in scope and more highly integrated internally.

Upgrading is obviously the opposite of downgrading; the risks of one are the benefits of the other. For example, upgraded workers know what symptoms mean and are more likely to take appropriate action, so the learning loop is strengthened. Overhead cost is lower because fewer middle managers and support personnel are needed. Placing the nonstructured work in the bargaining unit also fosters good union-management relations—even as this move is made possible by good relationships.

On the other hand, upgrading costs more in pay, heightens dependence on workers' competence and reliability, and makes a company more vulnerable to turnover among less easily replaceable workers.

In most plants we visited, management has concluded that the potential benefits outweigh the risks and has opted for upgrading. This trend is likely to grow as the importance of direct labor costs drops and professional and management payrolls rise. Improvements in worker-management and union-management relationships will also strengthen this pattern.

Supporting policies

Upgrading will not work without policies that breed loyalty and commitment from the work force. Here are some we saw at the plants we studied:

Employee involvement. Many factory managers have built commitment and loyalty by keeping workers up-to-date about plans for AMT, laying out the implications for job security and working conditions, and asking them to join in the project. An electronics components plant produced videotapes that showed automation making employees more effective and jobs easier. The tapes also underscored the threat of worldwide competition and linked the new machinery to the plant's nearly 30-year history of automation.

At several sites, workers accompanied managers on visits to equipment vendors and made suggestions for modifying equipment to meet their needs. At other plants, workers regularly helped supervisors establish procedures and improve operations, product quality, and the work environment. For example, the axle plant employees reviewed the lighting system and recommended extensive changes (later adopted) in the plant engineer's scheme. They also decided which of three shifts would be unstaffed.

At most companies, employees were deeply involved in the effort to change the plant culture. Supervisors were encouraged to be resources to workers rather than watchdogs, and status differences like attire, parking, and eating facilities were muted.

Employment continuity. Every plant had considered how to protect workers from AMT-related employment losses. Some companies, however, dealt with the issue more systematically than others. Policies included: promoting and training only from within; respecting seniority rights in interplant transfers and providing moving allowances; assigning employees to a 90-day trial at another plant and giving them the option to return to the original site if they found no appropriate niche; offering full pay and benefits during retraining to people laid off because of a change in technology; bringing subcontracted work back into the plant; and understaffing to reduce the likelihood of layoffs during downturns.

We concluded that an upgrading strategy cannot be fully effective unless planners give high priority to employment security. AMT's effects on employment tend to be mixed. On the one hand, fewer employees are needed with the new technology. On the other hand, unless AMT leads to heightened competitiveness, the number of jobs may decline even more. At a minimum, therefore, all parties must understand

Exhibit II **Aligning AMT and HRM**

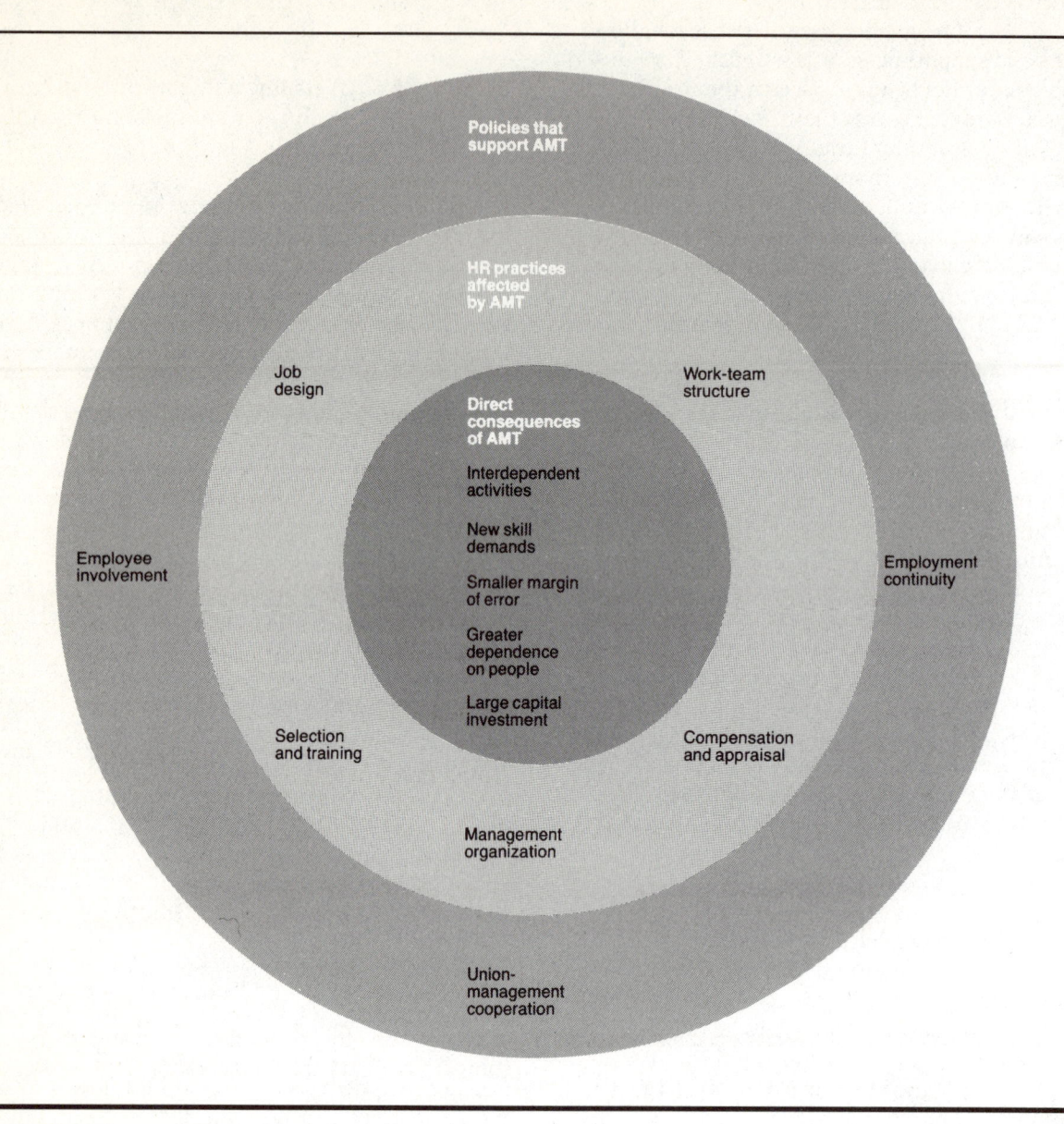

Policies that support AMT: Employee involvement, Job design, Work-team structure, Employment continuity, Compensation and appraisal, Management organization, Union-management cooperation, Selection and training

HR practices affected by AMT: Job design, Work-team structure, Compensation and appraisal, Selection and training

Direct consequences of AMT: Interdependent activities, New skill demands, Smaller margin of error, Greater dependence on people, Large capital investment

AMT's role in preserving or increasing market share and, consequently, jobs. At the same time, the policies that govern employment security and ease labor dislocations must be as favorable as the company's competitive circumstances permit, since AMT requires a solid foundation of human commitment and skills.

Union-management cooperation. Our site visits produced a good deal of evidence that unions as well as employers benefited from AMT. The company gained because it got better trained workers who could exercise good judgment in operating and maintaining expensive equipment. The union gained because its members got more secure employment, more interesting and challenging jobs, and higher pay. The plants varied in their ability to accommodate both parties' interests—but the important fact is that the two sides in most plants had sought win-win solutions. And the search itself created a favorable climate for change.

Successful implementation of AMT calls for a strong labor-management relationship. Indicators of such a relationship are management's willingness to notify the union about new technology as early as possible and readiness to involve the union in implementing it as fully as possible. In five organized plants we visited, union officers or members accompanied engineers on trips to vendors and recommended equipment to buy. In addition, the union acted as an advocate for the new technology because officials understood that in the long run it provided the only way for members to retain their jobs. If union members are kept in the dark about the technology until all key decisions have been made, however, the union is obviously much less likely to be an advocate.

Most of the unionized plants visited had experimented with labor-management cooperation before the advent of AMT. (Quality-of-work-life programs and joint committees were typical.) In some instances, moreover, management used the quality of its relationship with the unions as a consideration in its decision whether to introduce AMT in an established plant or at a greenfield site.

One of the most difficult issues in existing plants is the way union and management should deal with job classification reductions. Managers at three unionized plants agreed to create a new, higher paying classification for AMT jobs, primarily to prevent the occupants from being bumped during layoffs. Seniority was plantwide, so that workers with high seniority could bump down to lower rated jobs to avoid being laid off. The new job classification gave management some flexibility in assignment and assured workers of employment while they trained for AMT jobs. This arrangement does not reduce the number of job classifications in the plant, however. Also, only a few workers have flexible job assignments; most workers hold traditional jobs.

Another difficult issue concerned the integrity of the bargaining unit. Managements and unions have to agree on criteria for deciding who does what work. At several sites, both sides raised issues related to the blurring of boundaries between management and work-force responsibilities with AMT. Computer programming by production workers is a good example since the job blurs the boundaries between management and work-force responsibilities. At some companies, this was an issue; in others, it was not.

Aligning AMT & HRM

Our research offered enough data to create a composite or ideal human resource model derived from current best practice (see *Exhibit II*). The model can serve as a guide for managers contemplating the purchase or installation of AMT.

At the center of *Exhibit II* are AMT's first-order implications, the consequences that will follow directly from the decision to introduce new technology in the workplace. Some, like the degree of interdependence and the cost of a malfunction, also depend on how integrated the new technology is.

The middle ring identifies human resource policy considerations that AMT makes especially important. Some, like broader jobs and work teams, are adaptations of innovations from the 1970s, while others, like training and selection practices, have new urgency. What is striking is the degree to which these practices seem to be aligned with both the technology and progressive management philosophies.

Supporting policies of AMT are in the model's outer ring. Desirable in most contexts because they foster good working relations, they are prerequisites to the effective use of the middle-ring practices and to the introduction of AMT. Workplace changes of the magnitude of those occurring in these plants cannot succeed unless workers and their unions (if they are unionized) support them.

Managers planning to install AMT may want to start their analysis with its first-order implications, then explore new job designs, and finish by coordinating choices about other human resource practices and supporting policies. Implementation, however, may proceed in reverse, with supporting policies introduced first, to be followed by new personnel practices.

Some plants were more innovative than others; a few tried new policies in most if not all of the categories shown in *Exhibit II*. The most innovative plants were more likely to have a strategic rationale for investing in AMT as well as very high performance expectations—like better design, higher product quality, lower inventory, and improved cost performance.

Such expectations not only justify large capital investment but they are also necessary psychologically to inspire the organizational changes that will help realize the technology's potential. AMT can be the catalyst for breaking with tradition, for candidly examining habits, work rules, prerogatives, and relationships, and for assessing their adverse consequences for motivation, cooperation, and other factors that affect productivity. It can also encourage openness to learning from experience: we were struck by how many managers and union officials look enthusiastically at other companies, industries, and countries for implementation ideas.

Since we confined our research to plants that had introduced AMT recently, we cannot forecast what will happen next. Executives may consider downgrading once the technology is debugged and can take over still more of the functions that require operator discretion. Such an outcome is less likely, though, if managers decide to respect their human resources and encourage their development, and if they understand the reasons for aligning advanced manufacturing technology and innovative personnel policies.

We are convinced that managers who develop their human resources in conjunction with implementing AMT will achieve a competitive advantage. It takes many years to perfect and reinforce the practices we saw in these pioneering plants. But companies that are willing to take the time to lay this solid foundation will gain the edge in the long run.

Reprint 87215

SPECIAL REPORT

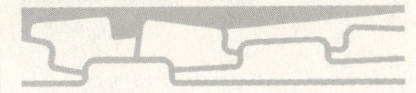

Greater employee responsibility does not mean greater discretion over time and work.

The Human Costs of Manufacturing Reform

by Janice A. Klein

If there is anything more powerful than an idea whose time has come, it is one that is the product of wishful thinking. Ask any manager or management consultant what the related essentials of manufacturing reform are, and the answer will likely come back: a just-in-time approach to eliminating waste, rigorous statistical process control to improve quality, and increased employee participation and self-management. One manager I know was emphatic: "JIT, SPC, and worker involvement in production management are like the three legs of a milking stool. Each is critical. If any one of the three breaks or is missing, the others will fall down."

He was an operations manager, eager to tap his workers' knowledge. He also anticipated their enthusiasm. It seemed obvious to him that increased participation was precisely what workers wanted or would quickly come to want. Implicit in that view is the belief that reformed manufacturing is more consistent with the moral ideal of "autonomy" than traditional manufacturing is.

Is it? That depends on what one means, precisely, by "participation": employee involvement, self-management, and teams. In the United States and Europe, most designers of employee participation programs think of teams as a way of *empowering* the work force. Companies involve workers in manufacturing reform by allowing team members a good deal of autonomy in managing daily activities—in scheduling the work and determining the procedures to carry it out.

In Japan, in contrast, where JIT and SPC have been used most extensively, employees are routinely organized into teams, but their involvement in workplace reform is typically restricted to suggestions for process improvement through structured quality control circles or *kaizen* groups. Individual Japanese workers have unprecedented responsibility. Yet it is hard to think of them exercising genuine autonomy, that is, in the sense of independent self-management.

To be sure, managers can—and must—involve workers in workplace decisions. But the attack on waste, it must be understood, inevitably means more and more strictures on a worker's time and action. Our conventional Western notions of worker self-management on the factory floor are often sadly incompatible with them.

The engine plant

Nothing brought this point home to me more graphically than the case of an engine plant I've studied. Over ten years ago, a large engine company designed a greenfield site; high among its priorities were worker morale and participation. The organizational design included self-managing work teams, many provisions for multiskilled workers, a reasonably flat—not hierarchical—management structure, and an explicit commitment to a "factory culture" based on growth, trust, equity, and excellence. Workers met schedules they themselves helped to set, laid out their work space to suit themselves, and performed assembly tasks in the manner they thought best. Meanwhile, inventory buffers provided time for workers to participate in management decisions. The plant soon became a model for the corporation, outperforming its traditional manufacturing operations not only in improved quality and safety but also in reduced overhead.

In the early days, the plant was not under severe cost or delivery pressures; the primary focus was on producing a top-quality product in an enriching work environment. But with the oil embargo, a recession in the automobile industry, and intensified foreign competition, the corporation found it necessary to reduce its manufacturing costs drastically.

Janice A. Klein is an assistant professor at the Harvard Business School. Her last contribution to HBR (with Pamela A. Posey) was "Good Supervisors Are Good Supervisors—Anywhere" (November-December 1986).

Top management believed that JIT and SPC would improve the company's competitiveness and quality and decided to introduce these approaches throughout the corporation's facilities.

The plant workers, who were by now accustomed to taking the initiative, quickly responded by forming a number of groups to plan the implementation process. One group began by scanning literature, attending seminars, and visiting other companies that had implemented JIT and SPC. A second focused on the plant's work flow, taking on the challenge of improving fixtures and tooling to reduce setups on individual work stations. (It videotaped the operations of all the teams, whose members then viewed the tapes and brainstormed to find ways of reducing "non-value-added" work.) After documenting all preliminary ideas, the team estimated savings from each policy and identified short-, medium-, and long-term goals. A third group ultimately carried out implementation: it planned the redesign of the shop and set the implementation schedule.

This is when the problems started. Management had expected smooth sailing because of the work force's flexibility. As one manager recalled: "When we decided to introduce JIT and SPC, we talked with others who had already implemented them to learn from their experiences. They all said you get increased commitment from employees. And they did not have as highly flexible work situations as we did." But as JIT and SPC began to take hold, employees began to complain that the plant's basic principle of employee involvement was being undermined.

In fact, workers were losing much of their freedom with the regimentation necessitated by JIT and SPC. Particularly vexing was the elimination of buffer inventory between, and within, work teams. Many workers and team managers began to voice concern: "We're losing our team identity and individual freedom with JIT." "Management is reverting to the traditional control mentality." "The shift in the plant is from a human focus toward more business basics for survival."

In retrospect, it is hard to believe that none of us saw this coming. True, under JIT and SPC, employees become more self-managing than in a command-and-control factory. They investigate process improvements and monitor quality themselves; they consequently enjoy immediate, impartial feedback regarding their own performance. (Managers don't have to tell them how they're doing. They help design the system, and *it* tells them how they're doing.) They also gain a better understanding of all elements of the manufacturing process.

On the other hand, the reform process that ushers in JIT and SPC is meant to *eliminate all variations within production* and therefore requires strict adherence to rigid methods and procedures. With JIT, workers meet set cycle times; with SPC, they must follow prescribed problem-solving methods. In their pure forms, then, JIT and SPC can turn workers into extensions of a system no less demanding than a busy assembly line. They can push workers to the wall.

Let us look more closely at what is lost.

Loss of individual autonomy. In a continuous-process operation, the coupling of worker and machine is limited by *machine* cycle time. Operators typically have a significant period to monitor dials or gauges, which may allow them a certain amount of slack time. Similarly, lengthy machine cycles often provide operators sufficient time to perform "vertical" tasks (administrative or other duties traditionally performed by supervisors or staff personnel) or to assemble for a team meeting.

In a nonautomated or barely automated assembly line, the limiting factor is *operator* cycle time. With JIT, buffers are reduced—as is slack and idle time. As a result, employees have less time, if any, for vertical tasks or team meetings. Operators in job shops, who are expected to run multiple machines, can conceivably have even less time than workers in assembly line operations.

Although JIT advocates argue that abolishing wasteful operations leads to more meaningful, effective work, there are in fact a number of reasons for higher stress levels among line operators under JIT. Under the Toyota Production System, for example, workers adhere to rigid cycle times and are expected to adjust immediately to changes as demand fluctuates.

At Toyota, a multiskilled operator attends to as many as 16 machines at once. The operator first picks up one unit brought from the preceding process and sets it on the first machine. At the same time, he (or she) detaches another piece already processed by this machine and puts it on a chute in front of the next machine. Then, while walking to the second machine, he pushes a switch to start the first machine. After performing a similar sequence on all 16 machines, the operator returns to the initial process. "This is done in exactly the cycle time necessary, perhaps five minutes, so one unit of a finished gear will be completed in five minutes."[1]

According to one informed observer, line operators at Toyota have claimed that the JIT pace led to "more major accidents (resulting in a loss of four or more days at work) than in other Japanese automakers and an unusually high number of suicides among the blue-collar work force." Officials deny such claims but do admit that they encountered startup problems: lack of skills in adjusting to different types of equipment and resistance to running multiple machines.[2] Incidentally, less severe but similar problems occurred at the engine plant, where there was an increase in the number of medical restrictions for working on the assembly line under JIT.

At the engine plant, finally, the inflexible pace of the line impaired motivation. As one manager commented: "Everyone is affected. If I were a person who liked to build a lot of engines and could work fast, the line used to be fun. It felt good, I accomplished a lot, and got a lot of satisfaction from it. Today, I am slowed down and bored. Or take a slow person, one who wasn't pushed at all by the old system. He would now have an awful lot of stress because he's really pacing the line. The entire day is very stressful."

Loss of team autonomy. Under JIT, individual team activities must be tightly coordinated with other teams in the production pipeline.

> Collaboration among work teams protects workers' self-esteem.

The loss of inventory buffers means that team meetings cannot simply be held whenever the need arises. Even coffee breaks must be coordinated across teams. As a result, individual team autonomy is replaced by carefully structured patterns of collaboration. Which is why team members at the engine plant complained that they had less freedom in solving problems; they felt limited in making process improvements because they believed they could only make changes that didn't affect other teams.

In addition, JIT drastically alters performance measurements. In traditional line flows, team members are typically given monthly stretch goals, as opposed to daily quotas. Under JIT, performance is measured against cycle goals. "It is not a 30-day time span, it is a 3-minute time span," noted one manager. Another put it this way: "It used to be that you had a monthly goal and you really shot for it. If you were down, you would have the business manager and the team manager—everyone working on the line—try to make the monthly goal. Now they have targets every day. It used to be that you could loaf a little bit, and other days you knew you were under the gun. Now you're under the gun all the time."

Loss of autonomy over methods. When the engine plant first started, teams had a great deal of autonomy in the improvement process. They had the freedom, within certain guidelines, to make changes on a trial basis; they were encouraged to be free-lancers, to take risks. As one team manager noted: "I was told in strong terms during the first several years I was here that I wasn't to do anything just because 'that's the way it's done.' I was told to do things the smartest way I could." Under JIT and SPC, this "entrepreneurial" spirit was limited; ideas are still encouraged but have to be tested under SPC guidelines.

Clearly, managers shouldn't give license to experiment where, in departing from established procedures, workers might jeopardize product integrity. But displacing worker trial and error with more scientific methods may have a negative psychological effect. Employees complained that SPC's structured experimentation restricted their freedom to make process changes. They perceived a loss of trust. As one manager noted: "It used to be that workers trusted us to listen to their ideas. Now we are troubleshooting more analytically and saying 'no' to workers more often than not. We say that their ideas don't fit SPC procedures. They say their ideas used to be worth something—now they are not."

Finally, SPC's process-capability studies may require operator certification programs. This is demoralizing for veteran workers. One worker responded to the certification process this way: "I can run every machine on this line, and I have done it on weekends, holidays, whenever. Now you say that I have to pass this road test to do it."

From autonomy to collaboration

What is to be done? Obviously, worker participation programs were never a carte blanche issued to operators to run production processes the way they wanted. The programs recognized axioms like concern for the customer, for the next team on the line, and for the schedule. Indeed, under JIT and SPC, tasks are more tightly coupled than ever before.

The key to protecting workers' self-esteem, then, is setting up a process for greater collaboration between teams—a time-consuming process, to be sure, but worth it in the long run. At NUMMI, the GM-Toyota joint venture, collaboration is now the name of the game. Whenever there is a cycle-time change (like when the plant went from a 54-second to a 68-second cycle time to accommodate slackening market demands), the teams have two to four weeks to plan changes in work station assignments. Teams have significant latitude in determining task sequences and work methods at each station; the team leaders (UAW working leaders) and group leaders (first-line supervisors) essentially become industrial engineers.

The objective is to balance the work load across all stations. This eliminates "cake jobs" and ensures that team members who rotate between stations within their teams can perform their tasks following standard procedures. When, for example, one team believes it would be better to reassign a particular task to another team—thereby changing the assembly sequence—all teams involved must reach a consensus.

Likewise, when a team member has a suggestion for improving a standardized job, a collaborative process begins again. The team member explains the idea to the team leader on that shift. If the team leader agrees that the idea has merit, the two try to sell it to their group leader. If the group leader likes it, then the three of them present it to the group leader and team leader on the other shift. Once there is a consensus at this level, the team members on both shifts are asked for input. If there is a problem, both shifts meet to try to gain consensus.

If there is agreement, the idea is ready for implementation. One shift will first try it out for approximately one week. During this period, the team leader, group leader, and quality assurance personnel evaluate the change, making modifications where necessary. If the idea works, it's instituted across shifts.

Again, process may appear tedious, but both managers and team members agree that the system has mitigated the frustrations that workers are apt to feel in such an interdependent system. It pushes joint responsibility and ownership for goals and objectives down to the teams and encourages their members, who cannot be wholly responsible for problem solving and designing work methods, to at least feel like participants. Needless to say, this is a far cry from the previous traditional management style at GM plants, where engineers dictated the work methods.

The only decision at NUMMI that might be considered completely at the discretion of individual workers is the pulling of the "andon," or line stop cord. However, even this initiates a collaborative process: when the cord is pulled, the team leader

> **Caution: The closer WIP inventory gets to zero, the more slack time you've eliminated.**

and the group leader quickly converge on the troubled work station to help solve the problem.

Tektronix also chose to emphasize the need for collaboration, but in a less structured way. For the assembly of one of Tektronix's portable oscilloscopes, a team of 35 assemblers and technicians broke into four subgroups: three feeder groups channeling work via a kanban system to a final assembly group. Individuals were free to change the procedure at their own work station, provided it did not affect any other work station. The revised procedure sheet informed anyone filling in at that station of any changes. (If a change affected the product in any way, the suggestion had to be reviewed with a team engineer.)

If any team member at Tektronix wanted to make a change that affected other members of the subgroup, for example, a change in the sequence of operations, the team member had to gain consensus from the group before making the change. If the change affected the entire team, however, the suggestion had to be raised at a weekly team meeting, where members would make a collaborative decision.

Here are other specific suggestions to mitigate the harsh effects of JIT and SPC:

Rethink zero inventory. In moving toward JIT, reducing inventory to an absolute zero level may not be the most economical or the wisest thing to do, at least not if it invites the system to break down.

The ultimate goal of JIT should be process control, not merely reducing inventory levels. NUMMI maintains a low level of "standard in-process stock" to balance the line and assure efficiency of the process. A minimum level of inventory may be justified to allow for team discussions or to alleviate individual employee stress. At the Saab-Valmet plant in Finland, for instance, buffers don't go below 20 minutes worth of work, because, as one of the managers put it, "Scandinavian respect for the workers' quality of life requires that the worker have the ability to work quickly for a few minutes in order to take a small personal break without stopping the line."[3]

Emphasize flow, not pace. Although JIT eliminates workers' ability to control their own work pace, using a kanban system allows workers to answer to each other rather than to a computer printout or supervisors. On the whole, kanban allows for more person-to-person initiative and communication. It therefore leads to a perception of increased worker control over the flow of production—though the reality may be otherwise. At Tektronix, for example, one team suggested increasing the kanban size to smooth

---

1. Yasuhiro Monden, *Toyota Production System: Practical Approach to Production Management* (Atlanta, Ga.: Industrial Engineering and Management Press, 1983), pp. 69-70.

2. Michael A. Cusumano, *The Japanese Automobile Industry: Technology and Management at Nissan and Toyota* (Cambridge: Harvard University Press, 1985), p. 305.

3. Suzanne de Treville, "Disruption, Learning, and System Improvement in Just-in-Time Manufacturing," unpublished dissertation, Harvard Business School, 1987.

production flow and still actually maintained daily output. If, however, too small a number of kanban squares allows for no buffer stock, the "human" system may prove even more stressful than any computerized one.

Focus on task design, not execution. Although there are limits on team freedom with respect to task execution, there is still room for

> **Workers who choose when to rotate tasks will feel freer.**

teams to be involved in task design. Teams can still have significant say regarding initial tooling and task sequence. Indeed, given the short product life cycles in many industries, production processes tend to be very dynamic; new products mean many new opportunities for employees to contribute to the work method. Of course, the excitement may wear off if the job becomes routinized over several months. It's important to allow for continual reassessment of the process.

Give workers the right to move and choose. As long as teams coordinate their activities with other teams, there is nothing to suggest that management must establish the times of breaks or "indirect" tasks. One might even argue that JIT and SPC give workers more opportunity to move around—to rotate between jobs or fill in wherever a problem arises. Such movement, of course, is not wholly discretionary. Workers must move where they are needed. Nevertheless, the sheer relief of changing tasks can make workers feel freer.

Furthermore, JIT and SPC do not restrict team autonomy with respect to assigning individual members to various tasks or determining job rotations. In some processes, team members may also be able to establish their own work hours, in accordance with a set flextime plan. At Tektronix, the first assemblers to arrive will fill their kanbans; if the assemblers in the following work stations have not arrived, the first assemblers will then rotate to the next station, working down the line until others arrive.

Teams can have significant autonomy in laying out the job. The technology will, in part, dictate the parameters. However, in many cases a team could simply be given the square footage available and a blank piece of paper to design its space.

Allow for workplace management of quality and resources. JIT helps to uncover the "rocks"—the bottlenecks and wasted motion—and SPC provides a tool for improving quality. Team members should be encouraged to reject incoming nonconforming materials and halt outgoing shipments of poor-quality goods. Teams can also continue to control quality through peer evaluations in performance ratings.

Moreover, work teams typically have access to and responsibility for securing the resources they need for their production goals. They may monitor and disperse resources within budget constraints, make staffing decisions, train new team members, and obtain assistance from support personnel. JIT and SPC in no way limit overall team autonomy in these areas, only the timing of these activities.

Managers experienced with JIT and SPC establish set times when teams and team members can perform such activities. Moreover, vertical tasks can be rotated among individual team members when production pressures require workers full-time on the line. Team meetings can be held during shift overlaps or when the line is shut down.

All such ideas require revising traditional performance measurement systems. Companies recognize the need to schedule downtime for preventative maintenance of machines. But preventative maintenance for people is just as critical. Employees need periodic relief—more frequently than a scheduled ten-minute break every two hours—especially as cycle times shorten. NUMMI plans for the line to be down 5% of the time as a result of line stops.

Managing expectations

If employees have never been given the latitude associated with self-managing work teams, their expectations tend to be lower. Hence many of the problems encountered by the engine manufacturer will not surface right away when JIT and SPC are introduced. But managers in high-commitment work systems particularly have to modify their workers' expectations without appearing to be reversing philosophy. This takes time. Time to teach, time to try to reach a consensus among workers that the changes associated with JIT and SPC are necessary.

As one manager at the engine manufacturer noted, "The teams feel like something was done to them, not with them. It is like having to get married, rather than wanting to get married." In the long run, a patient courtship will pay off.

> **Why promise more autonomy when you mean workers to deliver more cooperation?**

And aside from time, there is timing. If, for example, worker participation programs are implemented *after* JIT, there will be less confusion: workers will then not be invited to imagine greater freedom just when the new process takes freedom away. Even if some workers participate in the design of the system, this doesn't necessarily mean the plant will be operated by worker teams from the start. Besides, it is the task of managers, as always, to prepare the ground. They ought not to promise workers autonomy when they mean them to deliver an unprecedented degree of cooperation.

Reprint 89209

Good supervisors are good supervisors – anywhere

*Janice A. Klein
and Pamela A. Posey*

"Let's eliminate the first-line supervisors. Teams of workers can do the job just as well as the foremen, if not better. And we can reduce our indirect head count and get a cost savings too."

Comments like this were common not so long ago, when managers were talking about participative work systems. In theory they made sense, since these systems are designed to push the responsibility for production and quality down to the workers on the shop floor.

In practice, however, problems arose. Teams left to run their own shows often lacked direction. Team members didn't have the skills to solve many of the technical problems that arose and found it hard to get functional support. Many team members also balked at evaluating and disciplining their peers. At first the problems were ascribed to inexperience. But as time went on and teams matured, managers and workers had to admit that the old adage still holds, "Every team needs a coach."

> *"It's my job to know when I have to take the lead."*

What, exactly, does this mean? Are the "coaches" in participative organizations different from their peers in traditional systems? To test what we've observed in a number of manufacturing companies, we compared first-line supervisors in two plants owned by the same corporation. (See the insert for more information about the study.) One plant, which we'll call Kimball, is a high-commitment work site, organized and operated in a participative manner. The other, which we'll call Diamond, is a traditional, hierarchically designed and managed system. Our conclusion: a good supervisor is still a good supervisor. Top-notch performers do their jobs in much the same way, regardless of the work system or their formal titles.

Jobs change

To see just how different the supervisor's job is in a participative work system, let's look briefly at what Kimball requires of its first-line supervisors or team advisers as they're called at this plant.

According to their formal job description, team advisers are responsible for ensuring that the team has the resources it needs to make a quality product on time, representing the team in plantwide activities, developing the team and leading it in problem solving, motivating the team to achieve its goals, and assuming responsibility for indirect tasks. What this means in practice is that there is more emphasis on people than production, on relations than tasks. Team advisers have to be flexible enough in their methods to ensure that team learning occurs, perform a wide range of tasks, and meet plant performance goals. They must also be able to interpret the job description so that it accommodates both their individual styles and the needs of the team and others in the plant.

Janice Klein is assistant professor of business administration at the Harvard Business School, where she teaches production and operations management. Her previous HBR article, "Why Supervisors Resist Employee Involvement," appeared in the September-October 1984 issue. Pamela Posey is assistant professor of business administration at the University of Vermont, where she specializes in human resource management.

"Well, we merged and merged, then we divested and divested, and now here we are back again where we started, eh, fellas?"

Unlike their counterparts at Diamond, team advisers share responsibility with their teams for cost, quality, and on-time delivery of the product. So they must train their teams to manage the production process, including work assignments, and to solve the problems that crop up along the way, rather than provide solutions themselves. As one team adviser explained, "One of the hardest things to learn when I first came here was that I had the time to help the team learn from something that went wrong. I didn't have to take over. Back in Diamond I would have solved the problem myself and told the workers what to do. Here, that's their job."

Team advisers are also expected to manage the relations between their team and other company units (both production and support) and to get involved in plantwide activities like special task forces. As one team adviser described his job, "I have a lot of freedom here, freedom to get involved in activities that interest me. I can work on plant budgets or materials problems even though I am an assembly team adviser. Everyone here takes on some vertical tasks. We have our own assigned jobs, but we're expected to contribute to the plant as a whole, not just to our teams."

The latitude evident in this job description is reinforced by the plant's operating environment, which explicitly recognizes and rewards participation from all levels. Not surprisingly, however, this environment also reinforces a certain ambiguity about authority that is implicit in the team adviser's formal job description. In fact, team advisers do not always perceive that they have clear authority and control over their units. As one team adviser admitted, "Sometimes it's hard to remember that I really am the leader, the one with the power in this team. It's difficult to take control and act on your own when you are expected to pass responsibility and authority on to the team. Still, this isn't a democracy. It's my job to know whether my team has the skill to deal with a situation or whether I have to take the lead."

Ambiguity also cloaks the team adviser's responsibility for improving effort and output. Striving for improvement is an implicit and accepted part of the culture, so team advisers are responsible for motivating their workers and creating an environment that will encourage participation and individual development. At the same time, their own efforts outside the team can be directed anywhere—to special projects, to support teams, or to the plant as a whole. They must decide where they can contribute the most.

The contrast with traditional plants is instructive. At Diamond, the lines of authority are clear-cut. Supervisors know that when questions about performance or output arise, the buck stops with them. "I'm responsible for what comes out of this area," said one, "and I've been given the authority to make sure it's done right. If I have to sit on people to do that, then I sit on them. They know and I know I'm the boss."

Given these differences—in shop-floor organization, in authority structures, in job descriptions, and in the plants' informal operating environments—what differentiates the supervisors at Kimball from their peers at Diamond? For top performers the answer is, not much.

Performance stays the same

Outstanding team advisers at Kimball have the reputation for delivering what they say they will, and this gives them the credibility to shape performance. They understand team development in practical terms and share their skills and knowledge willingly with team members. They believe in and demonstrate power sharing, and they turn decision making into a learning experience for their teams. They view ambiguity and the lack of structure as a challenge, not a source of frustration, and they readily take control in a crisis, recognizing that they have the responsibility and authority to do so. Yet they are committed to the goals of teamwork and participation, and they find ways to foster them within the team and plant.

Outstanding supervisors at Diamond are strikingly similar. They too are characterized as competent, caring, and committed to both the work and their people. These supervisors push for quality, provide clear direction, and motivate their workers with timely and accurate feedback. They also tend to coach their workers and share information with them even though the system does not explicitly support participation. They take responsibility for the actions and outcomes of their units, know how to get the right people involved in the problem-solving process, and take the initiative to do so. Finally, like their counterparts at Kimball, they are the supervisors who look beyond their immediate areas to understand the plant and company as a whole.

Where we see a contrast, however, is within plants, between outstanding and average performers. Average team advisers understand team development in theory but have trouble translating it into practice. They maintain tighter control over their teams than their outstanding counterparts and are not fully comfortable with Kimball's participative processes. Average team advisers also tend to set narrowly defined goals and specific performance standards for their teams. They are less concerned with, or attuned to, the overall goals and needs of the plant and company. As a result, they do an adequate job but fail to develop a companywide perspective that would help them set broader, yet realistic, goals.

Average supervisors at Diamond are equally shortsighted and narrowly focused. They are viewed as directors, rather than coaches, and are less likely to provide regular feedback to their workers or share information routinely. They are less flexible, less innovative in their approach to problem solving, and slower to change. They are also less likely to initiate actions not demanded by the situation or to make decisions with incomplete information. In essence, they accept the system and its constraints as givens and rarely move beyond their confines.

These findings have important implications for managers in both traditional and innovative work settings because they debunk the myth that new systems require new and different supervisors. The supervisor's role in a participative system *is* different, as we've seen. But the behavior of successful first-line

Studying supervisors

While Kimball and Diamond differ in their work systems, their technology and production processes (components machinery and assembly) are closely matched. Diamond is the company's oldest facility and employs approximately 4,000 people. It is organized along business lines with distinct manufacturing functions operated semi-autonomously within the larger plant.

The five-layer management structure (plant manager, directors, business managers, unit managers, and supervisors) is common among traditional manufacturing plants. Production workers belong to an independent local union affiliated only with this corporation.

Kimball is a mature, high-commitment plant, acquired and brought on line in the early 1970s. It has about 1,000 employees. Kimball also uses the business concept, but it is organized around teams with every employee belonging to one. The management structure has four levels: plant manager, directors, business managers, and team advisers. (The team adviser position that focuses on facilitation rather than direction combines the supervisor and unit manager roles.)

Each business consists of direct production teams and support teams responsible for functions like set-up, maintenance, and materials handling. Production team members are expected to take on support responsibilities (quality control, finance, and staffing, for example) in addition to their basic duties, and these vertical tasks are an important part of the job. The plant is not unionized although it is located in a heavily unionized area.

We collected our data on supervisory performance from some 75 managers and supervisors during an 18-month period from late 1983 to early 1985. First, we held group interviews (6 at Kimball and 12 at Diamond) to identify plant-specific perceptions of the supervisory job and to isolate important performance criteria.

Next, we surveyed all the supervisors and production/operations managers at both plants to identify outstanding and average supervisors and explore performance differences between them. Each plant had its own survey. The response rate was 54% at Kimball and 43% at Diamond.

We then interviewed supervisors, both outstanding and average performers, from each plant individually (9 from Kimball and 10 from Diamond) and observed them during their regular work shifts.

supervisors—whether they're called foremen, coaches, coordinators, or team advisers—doesn't change. So we need to let common sense guide us in developing and implementing new work systems, especially when it comes to selecting and training supervisory personnel.

Selection. When looking for candidates to fit new systems, don't overlook your existing work force. Many supervisors are eager to apply their skills in nontraditional settings, and experience shows they deserve the chance. One company we know deliberately recruits its supervisors from older, traditional facilities because it wants people who are dissatisfied and eager to find a better way to manage.

> "It's time to debunk the myth that new systems require new and different supervisors."

Not all supervisors will make the transition successfully, of course. Indeed the "looseness" of new systems sometimes overwhelms average performers who need rigid rules and guidelines to fall back on when problems arise. But outstanding supervisors typically find it easy to transfer from traditional to new systems because they no longer have to work around a hierarchic structure to manage participatively. (In contrast, and counter to popular belief, supervisors who have been successful in new work systems often have a hard time moving to traditional plants because they are frustrated by their organizational rigidity.)

In choosing new supervisors, try to identify the criteria that led you to select your best performers in the past and apply them again. Interpersonal skills will count heavily, of course, as will technical knowledge. But whereas being a good coach was not an explicit prerequisite in the past, it probably should be today.

Training. When it comes to formal training programs, the old standards—group dynamics and problem solving—still apply. We do see a need, however, for more emphasis on group presentation skills and running effective meetings. Participative systems force supervisors to hold regular, formal meetings with their work groups. And while outstanding supervisors in traditional systems generally view their work groups as teams, they usually interact with them as individuals on a day-to-day basis. As a result, they may need to learn the skills that are necessary for managing group interaction.

Managers introducing participative work systems may also want to use some of their outstanding supervisors as role models and trainers. This approach has two advantages. First, pointing out these supervisors, identifying their performance as the goal, and structuring the organization to encourage behavior like theirs is much less threatening than saying that the supervisor's job has changed. So it may help to alleviate the fear many first-line supervisors feel when told that their companies are making a switch.

In addition, this approach will reinforce the fact that supervisors in new work systems must maintain their influence. This signal too often goes unsent when companies introduce participative work structures. Yet strong supervisors are especially desirable at this stage because team members lack technical and group problem-solving skills and require outstanding guidance. Once teams mature, however, they can often compensate for an average supervisor because they are better able to run themselves. And in some innovative plants, the teams even take on the job of training new or suboptimal supervisors.

In the past, first-line supervisors have often had to work around the system to be outstanding performers. Now we're developing systems that support their behavior. So let's not put them out to pasture just because they've only worked in traditional settings.

Reprint 86607

How one unorthodox company makes money by avoiding decisions, rules, and executive authority.

Managing Without Managers

by Ricardo Semler

In Brazil, where paternalism and the family business fiefdom still flourish, I am president of a manufacturing company that treats its 800 employees like responsible adults. Most of them—including factory workers—set their own working hours. All have access to the company books. The vast majority vote on many important corporate decisions. Everyone gets paid by the month, regardless of job description, and more than 150 of our management people set their own salaries and bonuses.

This may sound like an unconventional way to run a business, but it seems to work. Close to financial disaster in 1980, Semco is now one of Brazil's fastest growing companies, with a profit margin in 1988 of 10% on sales of $37 million. Our five factories produce a range of sophisticated products, including marine pumps, digital scanners, commercial dishwashers, truck filters, and mixing equipment for everything from bubble gum to rocket fuel. Our customers include Alcoa, Saab, and General Motors. We've built a number of cookie factories for Nabisco, Nestlé, and United Biscuits. Our multinational competitors include AMF, Worthington Industries, Mitsubishi Heavy Industries, and Carrier.

Management associations, labor unions, and the press have repeatedly named us the best company in Brazil to work for. In fact, we no longer advertise jobs. Word of mouth generates up to 300 applications for every available position. The top five managers—we call them counselors—include a former human resources director of Ford Brazil, a 15-year veteran Chrysler executive, and a man who left his job as president of a larger company to come to Semco.

When I joined the company in 1980, 27 years after my father founded it, Semco had about 100 employees, manufactured hydraulic pumps for ships, generated about $4 million in revenues, and teetered on the brink of catastrophe. All through 1981 and 1982, we ran from bank to bank looking for loans, and we fought persistent, well-founded rumors that the company was in danger of going under. We often stayed through the night reading files and searching the desk drawers of venerable executives for clues about contracts long since privately made and privately forgotten.

Most managers and outside board members agreed on two immediate needs: to professionalize and to diversify. In fact, both of these measures had been discussed for years but had never progressed beyond wishful thinking.

For two years, holding on by our fingertips, we sought licenses to manufacture other companies' products in Brazil. We traveled constantly. I remember one day being in Oslo for breakfast, New York for lunch, Cincinnati for dinner, and San Francisco for the night. The obstacles were great. Our company lacked an international reputation—and so did

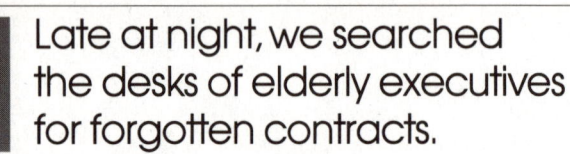

▎**Late at night, we searched the desks of elderly executives for forgotten contracts.**

our country. Brazil's political eccentricities and draconian business regulations scared many companies away.

Still, good luck and a relentless program of beating the corporate bushes on four continents finally paid off. By 1982, we had signed seven license agreements. Our marine division—once the entire company—was now down to 60% of total sales. Moreover, the managers and directors were all professionals with no connection to the family.

Ricardo Semler, 30, is president of Semco S/A, Brazil's largest marine and food-processing machinery manufacturer, and his book, Turning the Tables, *has been on Brazil's best-seller list for 60 weeks. He is vice president of the Federation of Industries of Brazil and a board member of SOS Atlantic Forest, Brazil's foremost environmental defense organization.*

With Semco back on its feet, we entered an acquisitions phase that cost millions of dollars in expenditures and millions more in losses over the next two or three years. All this growth was financed by banks at interest rates that were generally 30% above the rate of inflation, which ranged from 40% to 900% annually. There was no long-term money in Brazil at that time, so all those loans had maximum terms of 90 days. We didn't get one cent in government financing or from incentive agencies either, and we never paid out a dime in graft or bribes.

How did we do it and survive? Hard work, of course. And good luck – fundamental to all business success. But most important, I think, were the drastic changes we made in our concept of management. Without those changes, not even hard work and good luck could have pulled us through.

Semco has three fundamental values on which we base some 30 management programs. These values – democracy, profit sharing, and information – work in a complicated circle, each dependent on the other two. If we eliminated one, the others would be meaningless. Our corporate structure, employee freedoms, union relations, factory size limitations – all are products of our commitment to these principles.

It's never easy to transplant management programs from one company to another. In South America, it's axiomatic that our structure and style cannot be duplicated. Semco is either too small, too big, too far away, too young, too old, or too obnoxious.

We may also be too specialized. We do cellular manufacturing of technologically sophisticated products, and we work at the high end on quality and price. So our critics may be right. Perhaps nothing we've done can be a blueprint for anyone else. Still, in an industrial world whose methods show obvious signs of exhaustion, the merit of sharing experience is to encourage experiment and to plant the seeds of conceptual change. So what the hell.

Participatory Hot Air

The first of Semco's three values is democracy, or employee involvement. Clearly, workers who control their working conditions are going to be happier than workers who don't. Just as clearly, there is no contest between the company that buys the grudging compliance of its work force and the company that enjoys the enterprising participation of its employees.

But about 90% of the time, participatory management is just hot air. Not that intentions aren't good. It's just that implementing employee involvement is so complex, so difficult, and, not uncommonly, so frustrating that it is easier to talk about than to do.

We found four big obstacles to effective participatory management: size, hierarchy, lack of motivation, and ignorance. In an immense production unit, people feel tiny, nameless, and incapable of exerting influence on the way work is done or on the final profit made. This sense of helplessness is underlined by managers who, jealous of their power and prerogatives, refuse to let subordinates make any decisions for themselves – sometimes even about going to the bathroom. But even if size and hierarchy can be overcome, why should workers *care* about productivity and company profits? Moreover, even if you can get them to care, how can they tell when they're doing the right thing?

As Antony Jay pointed out back in the 1950s in *Corporation Man*, human beings weren't designed to work in big groups. Until recently, our ancestors were hunters and gatherers. For more than five million years, they refined their ability to work in groups of no more than about a dozen people. Then along comes the industrial revolution, and suddenly workers are trying to function efficiently in factories that employ hundreds and even thousands. Organizing those hundreds into teams of about ten members each may help some, but there's still a limit to how many small teams can work well together. At Semco, we've found the most effective production unit to consist of about 150 people. The exact number is open to argument, but it's clear that several thousand people in one facility makes individual involvement an illusion.

When we made the decision to keep our units small, we immediately focused on one facility that had more than 300 people. The unit manufactured commercial food-service equipment – slicers, scales, meat grinders, mixers – and used an MRP II system hooked up to an IBM mainframe with dozens of terminals all over the plant. Paperwork often took two days to make its way from one end of the factory to the other. Excess inventories, late delivery, and quality problems were common. We had tried various worker participation programs, quality circles, kanban systems, and motivation schemes, all of which got off to great starts but lost their momentum within months. The whole thing was just too damn big and complex; there were too many managers in too many layers holding too many meetings. So we decided to break up the facility into three separate plants.

To begin with, we kept all three in the same building but separated everything we could – entrances, receiving docks, inventories, telephones, as well as certain auxiliary functions like personnel, management information systems, and internal controls. We also scrapped the mainframe in favor of three independent, PC-based systems.

The first effect of the breakup was a rise in costs due to duplication of effort and a loss in economies of scale. Unfortunately, balance sheets chalk up items like these as liabilities, all with dollar figures attached, and there's nothing at first to list on the asset side but airy stuff like "heightened involvement" and "a sense of belonging." Yet the longer term results exceeded our expectations.

Within a year, sales doubled; inventories fell from 136 days to 46; we unveiled eight new products that had been stalled in R&D for two years; and overall quality improved to the point that a one-third rejection rate on federally inspected scales dropped to less than 1%. Increased productivity let us reduce the work force by 32% through attrition and retirement incentives.

I don't claim that size reduction alone accomplished all this, just that size reduction is essential for putting employees in touch with one another so they can coordinate their work. The kind of distance we want to eliminate comes from having too many people in one place, but it also comes from having a pyramidal hierarchy.

Pyramids and Circles

The organizational pyramid is the cause of much corporate evil, because the tip is too far from the base. Pyramids emphasize power, promote insecurity, distort communications, hobble interaction, and make it very difficult for the people who plan and the people who execute to move in the same direction. So Semco designed an organizational *circle*. Its greatest advantage is to reduce management levels to three – one corporate level and two operating levels at the manufacturing units.

It consists of three concentric circles. One tiny, central circle contains the five people who integrate the company's movements. These are the counselors I mentioned before. I'm one of them, and except for a couple of legal documents that call me president, counselor is the only title I use. A second, larger circle contains the heads of the eight divisions – we call them partners. Finally, a third, huge circle holds all the other employees. Most of them are the people we call associates; they do the research, design, sales, and manufacturing work and have no one reporting to them on a regular basis. But some of them are the permanent and temporary team and task leaders we call coordinators. Counselors, partners, coordinators, and associates. Four titles. Three management layers.

The linchpins of the system are the coordinators, a group that includes everyone formerly called foreman, supervisor, manager, head, or chief. The only people who report to coordinators are associates. No coordinator reports to another coordinator – that feature of the system is what ensures the reduction in management layers.

Like anyone else, we value leadership, but it's not the only thing we value. In marine pumps, for exam-

Our people often make higher salaries than their bosses.

ple, we have an applications engineer who can look at the layout of a ship and then focus on one particular pump and say, "That pump will fail if you take this thing north of the Arctic Circle." He makes a lot more money than the person who manages his unit. We can change the manager, but this guy knows what kind of pump will work in the Arctic, and that's worth more. Associates often make higher salaries than coordinators and partners, and they can increase their status and compensation without entering the "management" line.

Managers and the status and money they enjoy – in a word, hierarchy – are the single biggest obstacle to participatory management. We had to get the managers out of the way of democratic decision making, and our circular system does that pretty well.

But we go further. We don't hire or promote people until they've been interviewed and accepted by all their future subordinates. Twice a year, subordinates evaluate managers. Also twice a year, everyone in the company anonymously fills out a questionnaire about company credibility and top management competence. Among other things, we ask our employees what it would take to make them quit or go on strike.

We insist on making important decisions collegially, and certain decisions are made by a company-wide vote. Several years ago, for example, we needed a bigger plant for our marine division, which makes pumps, compressors, and ship propellers. Real estate agents looked for months and found nothing. So we asked the employees themselves to help, and over the first weekend they found three factories for sale, all of them nearby. We closed up shop for a day, piled everyone into buses, and drove out to inspect the three buildings. Then the workers voted – and they chose a plant the counselors didn't really want. It was an interesting situation – one that tested our commitment to participatory management.

The building stands across the street from a Caterpillar plant that's one of the most frequently struck factories in Brazil. With two tough unions of our own, we weren't looking forward to front-row seats for every labor dispute that came along. But we accepted the employees' decision, because we believe that in the long run, letting people participate in the decisions that affect their lives will have a positive effect on employee motivation and morale.

We bought the building and moved in. The workers designed the layout for a flexible manufacturing system, and they hired one of Brazil's foremost artists to paint the whole thing, inside and out, including the machinery. That plant really belongs to its employees. I feel like a guest every time I walk in.

I don't mind. The division's productivity, in.dollars per year per employee, has jumped from $14,200 in 1984 – the year we moved – to $37,500 in 1988, and for 1989 the goal is $50,000. Over the same period, market share went from 54% to 62%.

Employees also outvoted me on the acquisition of a company that I'm still sure we should have bought. But they felt we weren't ready to digest it, and I lost the vote. In a case like that, the credibility of our management system is at stake. Employee involvement must be real, even when it makes management uneasy. Anyway, what is the future of an acquisition if the people who have to operate it don't believe it's workable?

Hiring Adults

We have other ways of combating hierarchy too. Most of our programs are based on the notion of giving employees control over their own lives. In a word, we hire adults, and then we treat them like adults.

Think about that. Outside the factory, workers are men and women who elect governments, serve in the army, lead community projects, raise and educate families, and make decisions every day about the future. Friends solicit their advice. Salespeople court them. Children and grandchildren look up to them for their wisdom and experience. But the moment they walk into the factory, the company transforms them into adolescents. They have to wear badges and name tags, arrive at a certain time, stand in line to punch the clock or eat their lunch, get permission to go to the bathroom, give lengthy explanations every time they're five minutes late, and follow instructions without asking a lot of questions.

One of my first moves when I took control of Semco was to abolish norms, manuals, rules, and regulations. Everyone knows you can't run a large organization without regulations, but everyone also knows that most regulations are poppycock. They rarely solve problems. On the contrary, there is usually some obscure corner of the rule book that justifies the worst silliness people can think up. Common sense is a riskier tactic because it requires personal responsibility.

It's also true that common sense requires just a touch of civil disobedience every time someone calls attention to something that's not working. We had to free the Thoreaus and the Tom Paines in the factory and come to terms with that fact that civil disobedience was not an early sign of revolution but a clear indication of common sense at work.

So we replaced all the nitpicking regulations with the rule of common sense and put our employees

> **We wanted our workers to act like adults, so we stopped treating them like adolescents.**

in the demanding position of using their own judgment.

We have no dress code, for example. The idea that personal appearance is important in a job – any job – is baloney. We've all heard that salespeople, receptionists, and service reps are the company's calling cards, but in fact how utterly silly that is. A company that needs business suits to prove its seriousness probably lacks more meaningful proof. And what customer has ever canceled an order because the receptionist was wearing jeans instead of a dress? Women and men look best when they feel good. IBM is not a great company because its salespeople dress to the special standard that Thomas Watson set. It's a great company that also happens to have this quirk.

We also scrapped the complex company rules about travel expenses – what sorts of accommodations people were entitled to, whether we'd pay for a theater ticket, whether a free call home meant five minutes or ten. We used to spend a lot of time discussing stuff like that. Now we base everything on common sense. Some people stay in four-star hotels and some live like spartans. Some people spend $200 a day while others get by on $125. Or so I suppose. No one checks expenses, so there is no way of knowing. The point is, we don't care. If we can't trust people with our money and their judgment, we sure as hell shouldn't be sending them overseas to do business in our name.

We have done away with security searches, storeroom padlocks, and audits of the petty-cash accounts

Ricardo Semler's Guide to Stress Management

There are two things all managers have in common – the 24-hour day and the annoying need to sleep. Without the sleeping, 24 hours might be enough. With it, there is no way to get everything done. After years of trying to vanquish demon sleep and the temptation to relax, I tried an approach suggested by my doctor, who put it this way: "Slow down or kiss yourself good-bye."

Struck by this imagery, I learned to manage my time and cut my work load to less than 24 hours. The first step is to overcome five myths:

1. *Results are proportional to efforts*. The Brazilian flag expresses this myth in a slightly different form. "Order and Progress," it says. Of course, it ought to say, "Order *or* Progress," since the two never go together.

2. *Quantity of work is more important than quality*. Psychologically, this myth may hold water. The executive who puts in lots of hours can always say, "Well, they didn't promote me, but you can see how unfair that is. Everyone knows I get here at 8 A.M. and that my own children can't see me without an appointment."

3. *The present restructuring requires longer working hours temporarily*. We think of ourselves as corks on a mountain stream headed for Lake Placid. But the lake ahead is Loch Ness. The present, temporary emergency is actually permanent. Stop being a cork.

4. *No one else can do it right*. The truth is, you *are* replaceable, as everyone will discover within a week of your funeral.

5. This *problem is urgent*. Come on. The real difference between "important" and "urgent" is the difference between thoughtfulness and panic.

Those are the myths. The second step is to master my eight cures:

1. Set an hour to leave the office and obey it blindly. If you normally go home at 7:00, start leaving at 6:00. If you take work home on weekends, give yourself a month or two to put a stop to this pernicious practice.

2. Take half a day, maybe even an entire Saturday, to rummage through that mountain of paper in your office and put it in three piles.

Pile A: Priority items that require your personal attention and represent matters of indisputable importance. If you put more than four or five documents in this category and are not currently the president of your country, start over.

Pile B: Items that need your personal attention, but not right away. This pile is very tempting; everything fits. But don't fall into the trap. Load this stuff on your subordinates, using the 70% test to help you do it. Ask yourself: Is there someone on my staff who can do this task at least 70% as well as I can? Yes? Then farm it out. Whether or not your subordinates are overworked should not weigh in your decision. Remember, control of your time is an exercise in selfishness.

Pile C: Items that fall under the dubious rubric "a good idea to look at." One of the most egregious executive fallacies is that you have to read a little of everything in order to stay well-informed. If you

---

of veteran employees. Not that we wouldn't prosecute a genuinely criminal violation of our trust. We just refuse to humiliate 97% of the work force to get our hands on the occasional thief or two-bit embezzler.

We encourage – we practically insist on – job rotation every two to five years to prevent boredom. We try hard to provide job security, and for people over 50 or who've been with the company for more than three years, dismissal procedures are extra complicated.

On the more experimental side, we have a program for entry-level management trainees called "Lost in Space," whereby we hire a couple of people every year who have no job description at all. A "godfather" looks after them, and for one year they can do anything they like, as long as they try at least 12 different areas or units.

By the same logic that governs our other employee programs, we have also eliminated time clocks. People come and go according to their own schedules – even on the factory floor. I admit this idea is hard to swallow; most manufacturers are not ready for factory-floor flextime. But our reasoning was simple.

First, we use cellular manufacturing systems. At our food-processing equipment plant, for example, one cell makes only slicers, another makes scales, another makes mixers, and so forth. Each cell is self-contained, so products – and their problems – are segregated from each other.

Second, we assumed that all our employees were trustworthy adults. We couldn't believe they would come to work day after day and sit on their hands because no one else was there. Pretty soon, we figured, they would start coordinating their work hours with their coworkers.

limit the number of newspapers, magazines, and internal communications that you read regularly, you'll have more time to do what's important – like think. And remember to keep your reading timely; information is a perishable commodity.

3. In dealing with Pile A, always start with the most difficult or the most time-consuming. It also helps to have a folder for the things that *must* be done before you go home that day and to make a list of the things that simply cannot go undone for more than a few days or a week. Everything else is just everything else.

4. Buy another wastepaper basket. I know you already have one. But if you invited me to go through that pile of papers on your desk, I could fill both in a trice. To help you decide what to toss and what to save, ask yourself the question asked by the legendary Alfred P. Sloan, Jr.: "What is the worst that can happen if I throw this out?" If you don't tremble, sweat, or grow faint when you think of the consequences, toss it.

This second wastebasket is a critical investment, even though you'll never be able to fill both on a regular basis. Keep it anyway. It has a symbolic value. It will babysit your in-basket and act like a governess every time you wonder why you bought it.

5. Ask yourself Sloan's question about every lunch and meeting invitation. Don't be timid. And practice these three RSVPs:

"Thanks, but I just can't fit it in."

"I can't go, but I think *X* can." (If you think someone should.)

"I'm sorry I can't make it, but do let me know what happened."

Transform meetings into telephone calls or quick conversations in the hall. When you hold a meeting in your office, sit on the edge of your desk, or when you want to end the discussion, stand up from behind your desk and say, "OK, then, that's settled." These tricks are rude but almost foolproof.

6. Give yourself time to think. Spend half a day every week away from your office. Take your work home, or try working somewhere else – a conference room in another office, a public library, an airport waiting room – any place you can concentrate, and the farther away from your office the better. The point is, a fresh environment can do wonders for productivity. Just make sure you bring along a healthy dose of discipline, especially if you're working at home.

7. About the telephone, my practical but subversive advice is: Don't return calls. Or rather, return calls only to people you want to talk to. The others will call back. Better yet, they'll write, and you can spend ten seconds with their letter and then give it to the governess.

Two ancillary bits of phone advice: Ask your assistants to take detailed messages. Ask them always to say you cannot take the call at the moment. (Depending on who it is, your assistants can always undertake to see if you can't be interrupted.)

8. Close your door. Oh, I know you have an open-door policy, but don't be so literal.

And that's exactly what happened, only more so. For example, one man wanted to start at 7 A.M., but because the forklift operator didn't come until 8, he couldn't get his parts. So a general discussion arose, and the upshot was that now everyone knows how to operate a forklift. In fact, most people can now do several jobs. The union has never objected because the initiative came from the workers themselves. It was their idea.

Moreover, the people on the factory floor set the schedule, and if they say that this month they will build 48 commercial dishwashers, then we can go play tennis, because 48 is what they'll build.

In one case, one group decided to make 220 meat slicers. By the end of the month, it had finished the slicers as scheduled – except that even after repeated phone calls, the supplier still hadn't produced the motors. So two employees drove over and talked to the supplier and managed to get delivery at the end of that day, the 31st. Then they stayed all night, the whole work force, and finished the lot at 4:45 the next morning.

When we introduced flexible hours, we decided to hold regular follow-up meetings to track problems and decide how to deal with abuses and production interruptions. That was years ago, and we haven't yet held the first meeting.

Hunting the Woolly Mammoth

What makes our people behave this way? As Antony Jay points out, corporate man is a very recent animal. At Semco, we try to respect the hunter that dominated the first 99.9% of the history of our species. If you had to kill a mammoth or do without supper, there was no time to draw up an organization chart, assign tasks, or delegate authority. Basically, the person who saw the mammoth from farthest away was the Official Sighter, the one who ran fastest was the Head Runner, whoever threw the most accurate spear was the Grand Marksman, and the person all others respected most and listened to was the Chief. That's all there was to it. Distributing little charts to produce an appearance of order would have been a waste of time. It still is.

What I'm saying is, put ten people together, don't appoint a leader, and you can be sure that one will emerge. So will a sighter, a runner, and whatever else the group needs. We form the groups, but they find their own leaders. That's not a lack of structure, that's just a lack of structure imposed from above.

But getting back to that mammoth, why was it that all the members of the group were so eager to do their share of the work – sighting, running, spearing, chiefing – and to stand aside when someone else could do it better? Because they all got to eat the thing once it was killed and cooked. What mattered was results, not status.

Corporate profit is today's mammoth meat. And though there is a widespread view that profit sharing is some kind of socialist infection, it seems to me that few motivational tools are more capitalist. Everyone agrees that profits should belong to those who risk their capital, that entrepreneurial behavior deserves reward, that the creation of wealth should enrich the creator. Well, depending on how you define capital and risk, all these truisms can apply as much to workers as to shareholders.

Still, many profit-sharing programs are failures, and we think we know why. Profit sharing won't motivate employees if they see it as just another management gimmick, if the company makes it difficult for them to see how their own work is related to profits and to understand how those profits are divided.

> **After the hunt, primitive people shared their kill. Today's mammoth meat is profits.**

In Semco's case, each division has a separate profit-sharing program. Twice a year, we calculate 23% of after-tax profit on each division income statement and give a check to three employees who've been elected by the workers in their division. These three invest the money until the unit can meet and decide – by simple majority vote – what they want to do with it. In most units, that's turned out to be an equal distribution. If a unit has 150 workers, the total is divided by 150 and handed out. It's that simple. The guy who sweeps the floor gets just as much as the division partner.

One division chose to use the money as a fund to lend out for housing construction. It was a pretty close vote, and the workers may change their minds next year. In the meantime, some of them have already received loans and have begun to build themselves houses. In any case, the employees do what they want with the money. The counselors stay out of it.

Semco's experience has convinced me that profit sharing has an excellent chance of working when it crowns a broad program of employee participation, when the profit-sharing criteria are so clear and simple that the least gifted employee can understand them, and, perhaps most important, when employees have monthly access to the company's vital statistics – costs, overhead, sales, payroll, taxes, profits.

Transparency

Lots of things contribute to a successful profit-sharing program: low employee turnover, competitive pay, absence of paternalism, refusal to give consolation prizes when profits are down, frequent (quarterly or semiannual) profit distribution, and plenty of opportunity for employees to question the management decisions that affect future profits. But nothing matters more than those vital statistics – short, frank, frequent reports on how the company is doing. Complete transparency. No hocus-pocus, no hanky-panky, no simplifications.

On the contrary, all Semco employees attend classes to learn how to read and understand the numbers, and it's one of their unions that teaches the course. Every month, each employee gets a balance sheet, a profit-and-loss analysis, and a cash-flow statement for his or her division. The reports contain about 70 line items (more, incidentally, than we use to run the company, but we don't want anyone to think we're withholding information).

Many of our executives were alarmed by the decision to share monthly financial results with all employees. They were afraid workers would want to know everything, like how much we pay executives. When we held the first large meeting to discuss these financial reports with the factory committees and the leaders of the metalworkers' union, the first question we got was, "How much do division managers make?" We told them. They gasped. Ever since, the factory workers have called them "maharaja."

But so what? If executives are embarrassed by their salaries, that probably means they aren't earning them. Confidential payrolls are for those who cannot look themselves in the mirror and say with conviction, "I live in a capitalist system that remunerates on a geometric scale. I spent years in school, I have years of experience, I am capable and dedicated and intelligent. I deserve what I get."

I believe that the courage to show the real numbers will always have positive consequences over the long term. On the other hand, we can show only the numbers we bother to put together, and

> If executives are embarrassed by what they make, they probably aren't earning it.

there aren't as many as there used to be. In my view, only the big numbers matter. But Semco's accounting people keep telling me that since the only way to get the big numbers is to add up the small ones, producing a budget or report that includes every tiny detail would require no extra effort. This is an expensive fallacy, and a difficult one to eradicate.

A few years ago, the U.S. president of Allis-Chalmers paid Semco a visit. At the end of his factory tour, he leafed through our monthly reports and budgets. At that time, we had our numbers ready on the fifth working day of every month in super-organized folders, and were those numbers comprehensive! On page 67, chart 112.6, for example, you could see how much coffee the workers in Light Manufacturing III had consumed the month before. The man said he was surprised to find such efficiency in a Brazilian company. In fact, he was so impressed that he asked his Brazilian subsidiary, an organization many times our size, to install a similar system there.

For months, we strolled around like peacocks, telling anyone who cared to listen that our budget system was state-of-the-art and that the president of a Big American Company had ordered his people to copy it. But soon we began to realize two things. First, our expenses were always too high, and they never came down because the accounting department was full of overpaid clerks who did nothing but compile them. Second, there were so damn many numbers inside the folder that almost none of our managers read them. In fact, we knew less about the company then, with all that information, than we do now without it.

Today we have a simple accounting system providing limited but relevant information that we can

Ricardo Semler's Guide to Compensation

Employers began hiring workers by the hour during the industrial revolution. Their reasons were simple and rapacious. Say you ran out of cotton thread at 11:30 in the morning. If you paid people by the hour, you could stop the looms, send everyone home, and pay only for hours actually worked.

You couldn't do such a thing today. The law probably wouldn't let you. The unions certainly wouldn't let you. Your own self-interest would argue strongly against it. Yet the system lives on. The distinction between wage-earning workers and salaried employees is alive but not well, nearly universal but perfectly silly. The new clerk who lives at home and doesn't know how to boil an egg starts on a monthly salary, but the chief lathe operator who's been with the company 38 years and is a master sergeant in the army reserve still gets paid by the hour.

At Semco, we eliminated Frederick Winslow Taylor's segmentation and specialization of work. We ended the wage analyst's hundred years of solitude. We did away with hourly pay and now give everyone a monthly salary. We set the salaries like this:

A lot of our people belong to unions, and they negotiate their salaries collectively. Everyone else's salary involves an element of self-determination.

Once or twice a year, we order salary market surveys and pass them out. We say to people, "Figure out where you stand on this thing. You know what you do; you know what everyone else in the company makes; you know what your friends in other companies make; you know what you need; you know what's fair. Come back on Monday and tell us what to pay you."

When people ask for too little, we give it to them. By and by, they figure it out and ask for more. When they ask for too much, we give that to them too—at least for the first year. Then, if we don't feel they're worth the money, we sit down with them and say, "Look, you make x amount of money, and we don't think you're making x amount of contribution. So either we find something else for you to do, or we don't have a job for you anymore." But with half a dozen exceptions, our people have always named salaries we could live with.

We do a similar thing with titles. Counselors are counselors, and partners are partners; these titles are always the same. But with coordinators, it's not quite so easy. Job titles still mean too much to many people. So we tell coordinators to make up their own titles. They know what signals they need to send inside and outside the company. If they want "Procurement Manager," that's fine. And if they want "Grand Panjandrum of Imperial Supplies," that's fine too.

grasp and act on quickly. We pared 400 cost centers down to 50. We beheaded hundreds of classifications and dozens of accounting lines. Finally, we can see the company through the haze.

(As for Allis-Chalmers, I don't know whether it ever adopted our old system in all its terrible completeness, but I hope not. A few years later, it began to suffer severe financial difficulties and eventually lost so much market share and money that it was broken up and sold. I'd hate to think it was our fault.)

In preparing budgets, we believe that the flexibility to change the budget continually is much more important than the detailed consistency of the initial numbers. We also believe in the importance of comparing expectations with results. Naturally, we compare monthly reports with the budget. But we go one step further. At month's end, the coordinators in each area make guesses about unit receipts, profit margins, and expenses. When the official numbers come out a few days later, top managers compare them with the guesses to judge how well the coordinators understand their areas.

What matters in budgets as well as in reports is that the numbers be few and important and that people treat them with something approaching passion. The three monthly reports, with their 70 line items, tell us how to run the company, tell our managers how well they know their units, and tell our employees if there's going to be a profit. Everyone works on the basis of the same information, and everyone looks forward to its appearance with what I'd call fervent curiosity.

And that's all there is to it. Participation gives people control of their work, profit sharing gives them a reason to do it better, information tells them what's working and what isn't.

Letting Them Do Whatever the Hell They Want

So we don't have systems or staff functions or analysts or anything like that. What we have are people who either sell or make, and there's nothing in between. Is there a marketing department? Not on your life. Marketing is everybody's problem. Everybody knows the price of the product. Everybody knows the cost. Everybody has the monthly statement that says exactly what each of them makes, how much bronze is costing us, how much overtime we paid, all of it. And the employees know that 23% of the after-tax profit is theirs.

We are very, very rigorous about the numbers. We want them in on the fourth day of the month so we can get them back out on the fifth. And because we're so strict with the financial controls, we can be extremely lax about everything else. Employees can paint the walls any color they like. They can come to work whenever they decide. They can wear whatever clothing makes them comfortable. They can do whatever the hell they want. It's up to them to see the connection between productivity and profit and to act on it.

Reprint 89509

First Person
Firsthand lessons from experienced managers.

I wanted employees who would fly like geese. What I had was a company that wallowed like a herd of buffalo.

How I Learned to Let My Workers Lead

by Ralph Stayer

In 1980, I was the head of a successful family business—Johnsonville Sausage—that was in great shape and required radical change.

Our profits were above the average for our industry, and our financial statements showed every sign of health. We were growing at a rate of about 20% annually, with sales that were strong in our home state of Wisconsin and steadily rising in Minnesota, Michigan, and Indiana. Our quality was high. We were respected in the community. I was making a lot of money.

And I had a knot in my stomach that wouldn't go away. For one thing, I was worried about competition. We were a small, regional producer with national competitors who could outpromote, outadvertise, and underprice us any time they chose.

In addition to our big national competitors, we had a host of local and regional producers small enough to provide superior service to customers who were virtually their neighbors. We were too big to have the small-town advantage and too small to have advantages of national scale. Our business was more vulnerable than it looked.

What worried me more than the competition, however, was the gap between potential and performance. Our people didn't seem to care. Every day I came to work and saw people so bored by their jobs that they made thoughtless, dumb mistakes. They mislabeled products or added the wrong seasonings or failed to mix them into the sausage properly. Someone drove the prongs of a forklift right through a newly built wall. Someone else ruined a big batch of fresh sausage by spraying it with water while cleaning the work area. These were accidents. No one was deliberately wasting money, time, and materials; it was just that people took no responsibility for their work. They showed up in the morning, did halfheartedly what they were told to do, and then went home.

Now, I didn't expect them to be as deeply committed to the company as I was. I owned it, and they didn't. But how could we survive a serious competitive challenge with this low level of attentiveness and involvement?

Getting to Points B and A

In 1980, I began looking for a recipe for change. I started by searching for a book that would tell me how to get people to care about their jobs and their company. Not surprisingly, the search was fruitless. No one could tell me how to wake up my own work force; I would have to figure it out for myself.

And yet, I told myself, why not? I had made the company, so I could fix it. This was an insight filled with pitfalls but it *was* an insight: the fault was not someone else's, the fault was mine.

Of course, I hadn't really built the company all alone, but I had created the management style that kept people from assuming responsibility. Of course, it was counterproductive for me to own all the company's problems by myself, but in 1980 every problem did, in fact, rest squarely on my shoulders, weighing me down and—though I didn't appreciate it at the time—crippling my subordinates and strangling the company. If I was going to fix what I had made, I would have to start by fixing myself. In many ways that was my good luck, or, to put the same thought another way, thank God I was the problem so I could be the solution.

As I thought about what I should do, I first asked myself what I needed to do to achieve the company's goals. But what *were* the company's goals? What did I really want Johnsonville to be? I didn't know.

This realization led me to a second insight: nothing matters more than a goal. The most important question any manager can ask is, "In the best

---

Ralph Stayer is the CEO of Johnsonville Foods, Inc., of Sheboygan, Wisconsin and the managing partner of Leadership Dynamics, a consulting group that specializes in change.

of all possible worlds, what would I really want to happen?"

I tried to picture what Johnsonville would have to be to sell the most expensive sausage in the industry and still have the biggest market share. What I saw in my mind's eye was definitely not an organization where I made all the decisions and owned all the problems. What I saw was an organization where people took responsibility for their own work, for the product, for the company as a whole. If that happened, our product and service quality would improve, our margins would rise, and we could reduce costs and successfully enter new markets. Johnsonville would be much less vulnerable to competition.

The image that best captured the organizational end state I had in mind for Johnsonville was a flock of geese on the wing. I didn't want an organizational chart with traditional lines and boxes, but a "V" of individuals who knew the common goal, took turns leading, and adjusted their structure to the task at hand. Geese fly in a wedge, for instance, but land in waves. Most important, each individual bird is responsible for its own performance.

With that end state in mind as Point B, the goal, I turned to the question of our starting point, Point A. Johnsonville was financially successful, but I was dissatisfied with employee attitudes. So I conducted an attitude survey to find out what people thought about their jobs and the company and to get an idea of how they perceived the company's attitude toward them. I knew there was less commitment than I wanted, but I was startled all the same to find that Johnsonville attitudes were only average—no better than employee attitudes at big, impersonal companies like General Motors.

At first I didn't want to believe the survey, and I looked for all kinds of excuses. The methodology was faulty. The questions were poorly worded. I didn't want to admit that we had an employee motivation problem because I didn't know how to deal with that. But however strong the temptation, the mistakes and poor performance were too glaring to ignore.

The survey told me that people saw nothing for themselves at Johnsonville. It was a job, a means to some end that lay outside the company. I wanted them to commit themselves to a company goal, but they saw little to commit to. And at that stage, I still couldn't see that the biggest obstacle to changing their point of view was me. Everything I had learned and experienced to that point had convinced me that anything I didn't do myself would not be done right. As I saw it, my job was to create the agenda and then motivate "them" to carry it out.

In fact, I expected my people to follow me the way buffalo follow their leader—blindly. Unfortunately, that kind of leadership model almost led to the buffalo's extinction. Buffalo hunters used to slaughter the herd by finding and killing the leader. Once the leader was dead, the rest of the herd stood around waiting for instructions that never came, and the hunters could (and did) exterminate them one by one.

I realized that I had been focused entirely on the financial side of the business—margins, market share, return on assets—and had seen people as dutiful tools to make the business grow. The business *had* grown—nicely—and that very success was my biggest obstacle to change. I had made all the decisions about purchasing, scheduling, quality, pricing, marketing, sales, hiring, and all the rest of it. Now the very things that had brought me success—my centralized control, my aggressive behavior, my authoritarian business practices—were creating the environment that made me so unhappy. I had been Johnsonville Sausage, assisted by some hired hands who, to my annoyance, lacked commitment. But why should they make a commitment to Johnsonville? They had no stake in the company and no power to make decisions or control their own work. If I wanted to improve results, I had to increase their involvement in the business.

This was an insight that I immediately misused. Acting on instinct, I ordered a change. "From now on," I announced to my management team, "you're all responsible for

DRAWINGS BY WALLOP MANYUM

JOHNSONVILLE FOODS, INC.
COMPANY PERFORMANCE-SHARE EVALUATION FORM

Please check one: _____ Self _____ Coach

I. PERFORMANCE

A. Customer Satisfaction
How do I rate the quality of the work I do? Do I contribute my best to producing a product to be proud of–one that I would purchase or encourage someone else to purchase? Score _____

B. Cost-Effectiveness
To what extent do I perform my job in a cost-effective manner? Do I strive to work smarter? To work more productively with fewer errors? To complete my job functions in a timely manner, eliminating overtime when possible? To reduce waste where possible in all departments? Score _____

C. Attitude
To what extent do I have a positive attitude toward my personal, department, and company goals as expressed by my actions, feelings, and thoughts? Do I like to come to work? Am I thoughtful and considerate toward fellow members? Do I work to promote better attitudes? Do I demonstrate company loyalty? Score _____

D. Responsibility
To what extent do I take responsibility for my own job? Do I accept a challenge? Do I willingly take on or look for additional responsibilities? Do I work independently of supervision? Score _____

E. Ideas
To what extent have I offered ideas and suggestions for improvements? Do I suggest better ways of doing things instead of just complaining? Score _____

F. Problem Solver/Preventer
To what extent have I contributed to solving or preventing problems? Do I anticipate problem situations and try to avoid them? Do I push-pull when necessary? Do I keep an open line of communication? Score _____

G. Safety
To what extent do my actions show my concern for safety for myself and others? Do I alert coworkers to unsafe procedures? Do I alert my coach to unsafe conditions in my department? Score _____

H. Quality Image
To what extent have I displayed a high-quality image in my appearance, language, personal hygiene, and working environment? Score _____

---

making your own decisions." I went from authoritarian control to authoritarian abdication. No one had asked for more responsibility; I forced it down their throats. They were good soldiers, and they did their best, but I had trained them to expect me to solve their problems. I had nurtured their inability by expecting them to be incapable; now they met my expectations with an inability to make decisions unless they knew which decisions I wanted them to make.

After more than two years of working with them, I finally had to replace all three top managers. Worst of all, I now see that in a way they were right. I didn't really *want* them to make independent decisions. I wanted them to make the decisions I would have made. Deep down, I was still in love with my own control; I was just making people guess what I wanted instead of telling them. And yet I had to replace those three managers. I needed people who didn't guess so well, people who couldn't read my mind, people strong enough to call my bluff and seize ownership of Johnsonville's problems whether I "really" wanted to give it up or not.

I spent those two years pursuing another mirage as well–detailed strategic and tactical plans that would realize my goal of Johnsonville as the world's greatest sausage maker. We tried to plan organizational structure two to three years before it would be needed–who

II. TEAMWORK

A. Contribution to Groups
How would I rate my contribution to my department's performance? Am I aware of department goals? Do I contribute to a team? Do I communicate with team members?　　　　　　　　　　　　　Score _____

B. Communication
To what extent do I keep others informed to prevent problems from occurring? Do I work to promote communication between plants and departments? Do I relay information to the next shift? Do I speak up at meetings and let my opinions and feelings be known?　　　　　　　　　　　　　Score _____

C. Willingness to Work Together
To what extent am I willing to share the responsibility of getting the work done? Do I voluntarily assist others to obtain results? Do I demonstrate a desire to accomplish department goals? Do I complete paperwork accurately and thoroughly and work toward a smooth flow of information throughout the company? Am I willing to share in any overtime?　　　　　　　　　　　　　Score _____

D. Attendance and Timeliness
Do I contribute to the team by being present and on time for work (including after breaks and lunch)? Do I realize the inconvenience and hardship caused by my absence or tardiness?　　　　　　　　　　　　　Score _____

III. PERSONAL DEVELOPMENT

A. To what extent am I actively involved in lifelong learning? Taking classes is not the only way to learn. Other ways include use of our resource center or libraries for reading books, articles, etc.　　　　　　　　　　　　　Score _____

B. Do I improve my job performance by applying what I have learned?　　　　　　　　　　　　　Score _____

C. Do I ask questions pertaining to my job and other jobs too?　　　　　　　　　　　　　Score _____

D. Do I try to better myself not only through work but in all aspects of my life?　　　　　　　　　　　　　Score _____

E. Do I seek information about our industry?　　　　　　　　　　　　　Score _____

　　　　　　　　　　　　　TOTAL POINTS: _____

---

would be responsible for what and who would report to whom, all carefully diagramed in boxes and lines on charts. Later I realized that these structural changes had to grow from day-to-day working realities; no one could dictate them from above, and certainly not in advance. But at the time, my business training told me this was the way to proceed. The discussions went on at an abstract level for months, the details overwhelmed us, and we got nowhere.

In short, the early 1980s were a disaster. After two years of stewing, it began to dawn on me that my first reactions to most situations were usually dead wrong. After all, my organizational instincts had brought us to Point A to begin with. Pursuing those instincts now would only bring us *back* to Point A. I needed to start thinking before I acted, and the thought I needed to think was, "Will this action help us achieve our new Point B?"

Point B also needed some revision. The early 1980s taught me that I couldn't give responsibility. People had to expect it, want it, even demand it. So my end state needed redefining. The goal was not so much a state of shared responsibility as an environment where people insist on being responsible.

To bring people to that new Point B, I had to learn to be a better coach. It took me additional years to learn the art of coaching, by which, in a nutshell, I mean communicating a vision and then getting people to see their own behavior, harness their own frustrations, and own their own problems.

Early in the change process, for example, I was told that workers in one plant disliked working weekends, which they often had to do to meet deliveries. Suspecting that the weekends weren't really necessary, I pressed plant managers to use the problem as an opportunity. I asked them if they had measured production efficiency, for instance, and if they had tried to get their workers to take responsibility for the overtime problem. The first thing everyone discovered was that machine downtime hovered between 30% and 40%. Then they started coming to terms with the fact that all that downtime had its causes—lateness, absences, sloppy maintenance, slow shift startups. Once the workers began to see that they themselves were the problem, they realized that they could do away with weekend work. In three weeks, they cut downtime to less than 10% and had Saturdays and Sundays off.

Managing the Context

The debacle of ordering change and watching it fail to occur showed me my limitations. I had come to realize that I didn't directly control the performance of the people at Johnsonville, that as a manager I didn't really manage people. They managed themselves. But I did manage the context. I provided and allocated the resources. I designed and implemented the systems. I drew up and executed the organizational structure. The power of any contextual factor lies in its ability to shape the way people think and what they expect. So I worked on two contextual areas: systems and structures.

Systems. I first attacked our quality control system. Quality was central to our business success, one of our key competitive advantages. But even though our quality was better than average, it wasn't yet good enough to be great.

We had the traditional quality control department with the traditional quality control responsibilities—catching errors before they got to the customer. Senior management was a part of the system. Several times a week we evaluated the product—that is to say, we *checked* it—for taste, flavor, color, and texture.

One day it struck me that by checking the product, top management had assumed responsibility for its quality. We were not encouraging people to be responsible for their own performance. We were not helping people commit themselves to making Johnsonville a great company.

> Customer letters are answered by the line workers who make the sausage.

This line of reasoning led me to another insight: the first strategic decision I needed to make was who should make decisions. On the theory that those who implement a decision and live with its consequences are the best people to make it, we changed our quality control system. Top management stopped tasting sausage, and the people who made sausage started. We informed line workers that from now on it would be their responsibility to make certain that only top-quality product left the plant. In the future, they would manage quality control.

It surprised me how readily people accepted this ownership. They formed teams of workers to resolve quality problems. For example, one team attacked the problem of leakers—vacuum-packed plastic packages of sausage that leaked air and shortened shelf life. The team gathered data, identified problems, worked with suppliers and with other line workers to develop and implement solutions, even visited retail stores to find out how retailers handled the product so we could make changes that would prevent their problems from occurring. The team took complete responsibility for measuring quality and then used those measurements to improve production processes. They owned and expected to own all the problems of producing top-quality sausage, and they wanted to do the best possible job. The results were amazing. Rejects fell from 5% to less than 0.5%.

Clearly this new quality control system was helping to create the end state we were after. Its success triggered changes in several other systems as well.

Teams of workers in other areas began to taste the product every morning and discuss possible improvements. They asked for information about costs and customer reactions, and we redesigned the information system to give it to them.

We began to forward customer letters directly to line workers. They responded to customer complaints and sent coupons for free Johnsonville sausage when they felt it was warranted. They came to own and expect responsibility for correcting the problems that customers raised in their letters.

People in each section on the shop floor began to collect data about labor costs, efficiency, and yield. They posted the data and discussed it at the daily tasting meeting. Increasingly, people asked for more responsibility, and the information system encouraged them to take it. We were progressing toward our end state, and as we made progress we uncovered deeper and more complex problems.

One of these arose when people on the shop floor began to complain about fellow workers whose performance was still slipshod or indifferent. In fact, they came to senior management and said, "You don't take your own advice. If you did, you wouldn't let these poor performers work here. It's your job to either fix them or fire them."

Our first reaction was to jump in and do something, but by now we had learned to think before acting. We asked ourselves if accepting responsibility for this problem would help us reach Point B. The answer was clearly no. More important, we asked ourselves who was in the best position to own the problem and came to the obvious conclusion that the people on the shop floor knew more about shop-floor performance

How Johnsonville Shares Profits on the Basis of Performance

Every six months, we evaluate the performance of everyone at Johnsonville to help us compute shares in our profit-sharing program. Except "we" is the wrong word. In practice, performance evaluations are done by the employees themselves. For example, 300 wage earners—salaried employees have a separate profit-sharing pool and a different evaluation system—fill out forms in which they rate themselves on a scale of 1 to 9 in 17 specific areas grouped into three categories: performance, teamwork, and personal development.

Scores of 3, 4, or 5—the average range—are simply entered on the proper line. Low scores of 1 or 2 and high scores of 6 to 9 require a sentence or two of explanation.

Each member's coach fills out an identical form, and later both people sit down together and discuss all 17 areas. In cases of disagreement, the rule is only that their overall point totals must agree within nine points, whereupon the two totals are averaged to reach a final score. If they cannot narrow the gap to nine points, an arbitration group is ready to step in and help, but so far mediation has never been needed.

All final scores, names deleted, are then passed to a profit-sharing team that carves out five categories of performance: a small group of superior performers (about 5% of the total), a larger group of better-than-average workers (roughly 20%), an average group amounting to about 50% of the total work force, a below-average group of 20%, and a small group of poor performers who are often in some danger of losing their jobs.

The total pool of profits to be shared is then divided by the number of workers to find an average share—for the purpose of illustration, let's say $1,000. Members of the top group get a check for 125% of that amount or $1,250. Members of the next group get 110% ($1,100), of the large middle group, 100% or $1,000, and so on down to $900 and $750.

Yes, people do complain from time to time, especially if they think they've missed a higher share by only a point or two. The usual way of dealing with such situations is to help the individual improve his or her performance in enough areas to ensure a higher score the next time. But overall satisfaction with the system is very high, partly because fellow workers invented it, administer it, and constantly revise it in an effort to make it more equitable. The person currently in charge of the Johnsonville profit-sharing team is an hourly worker from the shipping department.

Many forms have been used over the years—a new one is under consideration at this moment—but the questions most recently asked, in a slightly edited version, are reprinted in this article.

---

than we did, so they were the best ones to make these decisions.

We offered to help them set performance standards and to coach them in confronting poor performers, but we insisted that since they were the production-performance experts, it was up to them to deal with the situation. I bit my tongue time and time again, but they took on the responsibility for dealing with performance problems and actually fired individuals who wouldn't perform up to the standards of their teams.

This led to a dramatic change in Johnsonville's human resource system. Convinced that inadequate selection and training of new workers caused performance problems, line workers asked to do the selection and training themselves. Managers helped them set up selection and training procedures, but production workers made them work. Eventually, line workers assumed most of the traditional personnel functions.

The compensation system was another early target for change. We had traditionally given across-the-board annual raises like most other businesses. What mattered was longevity, not performance. That system was also a stumbling block on our way to Point B, so we made two changes.

First, we eliminated the annual across-the-board raise and substituted a pay-for-responsibility system. As people took on new duties—budgeting, for instance, or training—they earned additional base income. Where the old system rewarded people for hanging around, regardless of what they contributed, the new one encouraged people to seek responsibility.

Second, we instituted what we called a "company performance share," a fixed percentage of pretax profits to be divided every six months among our employees. We based individual shares on a performance-appraisal system designed and administered by a volunteer team of line production workers from various departments. The system is explained in the insert "How Johnsonville Shares Profits on the Basis of Performance."

These system changes taught me two more valuable lessons. First, just start. Don't wait until you have all the answers. When I set out to make these changes, I had no clear picture of how these new systems would interact with one another or with other company systems and procedures, but if I had waited until I had all the answers, I'd still be waiting. A grand plan was impossible; there were too many variables. I wasn't certain which systems to change; I just knew I had to change something in order to alter expectations and begin moving toward my goal.

Second, start by changing the most visible system you directly control. You want your first effort to succeed. I knew I could control who tasted the product because I was doing the tasting. I also knew it was a highly visible action. Everyone waited to hear my taste-test results. By announcing that I wasn't going to taste the product anymore and that the people who made it were, everyone knew immediately that I was serious about spreading responsibility.

Structures. Along with the system changes, I introduced a number of changes in company structure. Teams gradually took over a number of the functions previously performed by individual managers in the chain of command, with the result that the number of hierarchical layers went from six to three.

Teams had already taken on responsibility for selecting, training, evaluating, and, when necessary, terminating fellow employees. Now they began to make all decisions about schedules, performance standards, assignments, budgets, quality measures, and capital improvements as well. In operations, teams assumed the supervisors' functions, and those jobs disappeared. Those former supervisors who needed authority in order to function left the company, but most went into other jobs at Johnsonville, some of them into technical positions.

The function of the quality control department was redefined. It stopped checking quality—now done by line workers—and began providing technical support to the production people in a cooperative effort to *improve* quality. The department developed systems for continuous on-line monitoring of fat, moisture, and protein content, for example, and it launched a program of outside taste testing among customers.

The traditional personnel department disappeared and was replaced by a learning and personal development team to help individual employees develop their own Points B and A—their destinations and starting points—and figure out how to use Johnsonville to reach their goals. We set up an educational allowance for each person, to be used however the individual saw fit. In the beginning, some took cooking or sewing classes; a few took flying lessons. Over time, however, more and more of the employees focused on job-related learning. Today more than 65% of all the people at Johnsonville are involved in some type of formal education.

The end state we all now envision for Johnsonville is a company that never stops learning. One part of learning is the acquisition of facts and knowledge—about accounting, machine maintenance, marketing, even about sky diving and Italian cooking. But the most important kind of learning teaches us to question our own actions and behavior in order to better understand the ways we perform, work, and live.

Helping human beings fulfill their potential is of course a moral responsibility, but it's also good business. Life is aspiration. Learning, striving people are happy people and good workers. They have initiative and imagination, and the companies they work for are rarely caught napping.

Learning is change, and I keep learning and relearning that change is and needs to be continuous. For example, our system and structural changes were reciprocal. The first led to the second, which then in turn led to new versions of the first.

Initially, I had hoped the journey would be as neat and orderly as it now appears on paper. Fortunately—since original mistakes are an important part of learning—it wasn't. There were lots of obstacles and challenges, much backsliding, and myriad false starts and wrong decisions.

For example, team leaders chosen by their team members were supposed to function as communication links, leaving the traditional management functions of planning and scheduling to the group itself. No sooner had the team leaders been appointed, however, than they began to function as supervisors. In other words, they immediately fell into the familiar roles they had always seen.

We had neglected to give them and the plant managers adequate training in the new team model. The structure changed, but mind-sets didn't. It was harder to alter people's expectations than I had realized.

Influencing Expectations

I discovered that change occurs in fits and starts, and that while I could plan individual changes and events, I couldn't plan the whole process. I also learned that expectations have a way of becoming reality, so I tried to use every available means—semantic, symbolic, and behavioral—to send messages that would shape expectations to Johnsonville's advantage.

For example, we wanted to break down the traditional pictures in people's minds of what managers do and how subordinates and employees behave, so we changed the words we used. We dropped the words employee and subordinate. Instead we called everyone a "member" of the organization, and managers became "coordinators" or "coaches."

Our promotion system had always sent a powerful message: to move up the ladder you need to become a manager and solve problems for your people. But this was now the wrong message. I wanted coordinators who could build problem-solving capaci-

> **The CEO who knows about a problem owns it. My advice: don't ask.**

ties in others rather than solve their problems for them. I recast the job requirements for the people whose work I directly coordinated (formerly known as "my management team"), and they, in turn, did the same for the people whose work they coordinated. I took every opportunity to stress the need for coaching skills, and I continually de-emphasized technical experience. Whenever someone became a coordinator, I made sure word got around that the promotion was for demonstrated abilities as a teacher, coach, and facilitator.

This new promotion standard sent a new message: to get ahead at Johnsonville, you need a talent for cultivating and encouraging problem solvers and responsibility takers.

I discovered that people watched my every action to see if it supported or undermined our vision. They wanted to see if I practiced what I preached. From the outset I did simple things to demonstrate my sincerity. I made a sign for my desk that said THE QUESTION IS THE ANSWER, and when people came to me with questions, I asked myself if they were questions I should answer. Invariably, they weren't. Invariably, people were asking me to make decisions for them. Instead of giving answers, I turned the tables and asked the questions myself, trying to make them repossess their own problems. Owning problems was an important part of the end state I'd envisioned. I wasn't about to let people give theirs to me.

I also discovered that in meetings people waited to hear my opinion before offering their own. In the beginning, I insisted they say what they thought, unaware that I showed my own preferences in subtle ways—my tone of voice, the questions I asked—which, nevertheless, anyone could read and interpret expertly. When I realized what was happening, I began to stay silent to avoid giving any clue to where I stood. The result was that people flatly refused to commit themselves to any decision at all. Some of those meetings would have gone on for days if I hadn't forced people to speak out before they'd read my mind.

In the end, I began scheduling myself out of many meetings, forcing others to make their decisions without me. I also stopped collecting data about production problems. I learned that if I had information about daily shortages and yields, I began to ask questions that put me firmly back in possession of the problems.

Eventually, I came to understand that everything I did and said had a symbolic as well as a literal meaning. I had to anticipate the potential impact of every word and act, ask myself again and again if what I was about to do or say would reinforce the vision or undermine it, bring us closer to Point B or circle us back to Point A, encourage people to own their own problems or palm them off on me. My job, as I had come to see it, was to put myself out of a job.

Watershed

By mid-1985, we had all come a long way. Johnsonville members had started wanting and expecting responsibility for their own performance, and they usually did a good job. Return on assets was up significantly, as were margins and quality. But on the whole, the process of change had been a journey without any major mileposts or station stops.

> **Palmer's contract offer was close to a bet-the-company decision.**

Then Palmer Sausage (not its real name) came along and gave us our watershed—a golden opportunity and a significant threat to our existence.

Palmer is a much larger sausage company that had contracted with us for private-label products during a strike in the early 1980s. Our quality was so high that they kept us on as a supplier after the strike ended. Now Palmer had decided to consolidate several facilities and offered to let us take over part of the production of a plant they were closing. It represented a huge increase in their order, and the additional business was very tempting: it could be very profitable, and it would justify the cost of a new and more efficient plant of our own. The upside was extremely attractive—if we could handle it.

That was what worried me. To handle an expanded Palmer contract, we'd have to hire and train a large group of people quickly and teach our present people new skills, keep quality high on both the Palmer products and our own, work six and seven days a week for more than a year until our new plant was ready, and run the risk if Palmer cancelled – which it could do on 30-days notice – of saddling ourselves with big layoffs and new capacity we no longer had a market for. Maybe it wasn't a bet-the-company decision, but it was as close as I'd like to come.

Before 1982, I would have met for days with my senior team to discuss all these issues, and we would probably have turned down the opportunity in the face of such an overwhelming downside. But by 1985, it was clear to me that the executive group was the wrong group to make this decision. The executives would not be responsible for successfully implementing such a move. The only way we could do Palmer successfully was if everyone at Johnsonville was committed to making it work, so everyone had to decide.

Until that moment, my senior team had always made the strategic decisions. We took advice from people in the operating departments, but the senior staff and I had dealt with the ultimate problems and responsibilities. We needed to move to a new level. This was a problem all of our people had to own.

My senior managers and I called a meeting of the entire plant, presented the problem, and posed three questions. What will it take to make it work? Is it possible to reduce the downside? Do we want to do it?

We asked the teams in each area to discuss these questions among themselves and develop a list of pros and cons. Since the group as a whole was too large to work together effectively, each team chose one member to report its findings to a plantwide representative body to develop a plantwide answer.

The small groups met almost immediately, and within days their representatives met. The discussion moved back and forth several times between the representative body and the smaller groups.

To make it work, the members decided we'd have to operate seven days a week, hire and train people to take new shifts, and increase efficiency to get more from current capacity. They also thought about the downside risk. The biggest danger was that we'd lose the added business after making all the investments and sacrifices needed to handle it. They figured the only way to reduce that downside potential was to achieve quality standards so high that we would actually improve the already first-rate Palmer product and, at the same time, maintain standards on our own products to make sure Johnsonville brands didn't fall by the wayside.

Ralph Stayer's Guide to Improving Performance

Getting better performance from any group or individual, yourself included, means a permanent change in the way you think and run your business. Change of this kind is not a single transaction but a journey, and the journey has a specific starting point and a clear destination.

The journey is based on six observations about human behavior that I didn't fully grasp when I started, though I'd have made faster progress and fewer mistakes if I had.

1. People want to be great. If they aren't, it's because management won't let them be.
2. Performance begins with each individual's expectations. Influence what people expect and you influence how people perform.
3. Expectations are driven partly by goals, vision, symbols, semantics, and partly by the context in which people work, that is, by such things as compensation systems, production practices, and decision-making structures.
4. The actions of managers shape expectations.
5. Learning is a process, not a goal. Each new insight creates a new layer of potential insights.
6. The organization's results reflect me and my performance. If I want to change the results, I have to change myself first. This is particularly true for me, the owner and CEO, but it is equally true for every employee.

So to make the changes that will lead to great performance, I recommend focusing on goals, expectations, contexts, actions, and learning. Lee Thayer, a humanities professor at the University of Wisconsin, has another way of saying pretty much the same thing. He argues that since performance is the key to organizational success, management's job is to establish the conditions under which superb performance serves both the company's and the individual's best interests.

CEOs need to focus first on changing themselves before they try to change the rest of the company. The process resembles an archaeological dig, or at least it did for me. As I uncovered and solved one problem, I almost invariably exposed another, deeper problem. As I gained one insight and mastered one situation, another situation arose that required new insight and more learning. As I approached one goal, a new, more important, but more distant goal always began to take shape.

Two weeks later, the company decided almost unanimously to take the business. It was one of the proudest moments of my life. Left to our traditional executive decision making, we would have turned Palmer down. The Johnsonville people, believing in themselves, rose to the challenge. They really did want to be great.

The results surpassed our best projections. Learning took place faster than anticipated. Quality rose in our own product line as well as for Palmer. The new plant came on line in 1987. Palmer has come back to us several times since to increase the size of its orders even further.

Success – The Greatest Enemy

The pace of change increased after Palmer. Now that all of Johnsonville's people expected and wanted some degree of responsibility for strategic decisions, we had to redefine Point A, our current situation. The new level of involvement also led us to a more ambitious view of what we could ultimately achieve – Point B, our vision and destination.

We made additional changes in our career-tracking system. In our early enthusiasm, we had played down the technical aspects of our business, encouraging everyone to become a coordinator, even those who were far better suited to technical specialties. We also had some excellent salespeople who became coordinators because they saw it as the only path to advancement, though their talents and interests lay much more in selling than in coaching. When they became coordinators, we lost in three ways: we lost good salespeople, we created poor coordinators, and we lost sales from other good salespeople because they worked for these poor coordinators.

A career team recommended that Johnsonville set up dual career tracks – one for specialists and one for coordinators – that would enable both to earn recognition, status, and compensation on the basis of performance alone. The team, not the senior coordinators, agreed to own and fix the compensation problem.

Everyone at Johnsonville discovered they could do considerably better and earn considerably more than they had imagined. Since they had little trouble meeting the accelerated production goals that they themselves had set, members raised the minimum acceptable performance criteria and began routinely to expect more of themselves and others.

Right now, teams of Johnsonville members are meeting to discuss next year's capital budget, new product ideas, today's production schedule, and yesterday's quality, cost, and yield. More important, these same teams are redesigning their systems and structures to manage their continuing journey toward Point B,

> **For the last five years, my ambition has been to eliminate my job.**

which, along with Point A, they are also continually redefining. Most important of all, their general level of commitment is now as high or higher than my own.

In fact, our greatest enemy now is our success. Our sales, margins, quality, and productivity far exceed anything we could have imagined in 1980. We've been studied and written about, and we've spent a lot of time answering questions and giving advice. We've basked in the limelight, telling other people how we did it. All the time we kept telling ourselves, "We can't let this go to our heads." But of course it had already gone to our heads. We had begun to talk and brag about the past instead of about what we wanted for the future. Once we saw what we were doing, we managed to stop and, in the process, learn a lesson about the hazards of self-congratulation.

Author's note: I wish to acknowledge the contribution of my partner, James A. Belasco, to this article.

When I began this process of change ten years ago, I looked forward to the time when it would all be over and I could get back to my real job. But I've learned that change *is* the real job of every effective business leader because change is about the present and the future, not about the past. There is no end to change. This story is only an interim report.

Yet another thing I've learned is that the cause of excitement at Johnsonville Sausage is not change itself but the process used in producing change. Learning and responsibility are invigorating, and aspirations make our hearts beat. For the last five years, my own aspiration has been to eliminate *my* job by creating such a crowd of self-starting, problem-solving, responsibility-grabbing, independent thinkers that Johnsonville would run itself.

Two years ago, I hired a new chief operating officer and told him he should lead the company and think of me as his paid consultant. Earlier this year, he invited me to a management retreat, and I enjoyed myself. Other people owned the problems that had once been mine. My whole job was to generate productive conversations about Johnsonville's goals and to communicate its vision.

On the second evening of the retreat, I was given a message from my COO. There was a special session the next morning, he wrote, and added, "I want you there at 8:15." Instinctively, it made me mad. Johnsonville was my company; I built it; I fixed it; he owed me his job. Who the hell did he think he was giving me orders like a hired consultant?

Then, of course, I laughed. It's not always easy giving up control, even when it's what you've worked toward for ten years. He wanted me there at 8:15? Well, good for him. I'd be there.

Reprint 90610

• SPECIAL COLLECTIONS • BOOKS • HBR ARTICLES • CUSTOM HBR ARTICLES • VIDEOS • CASES •

READ THE FINE PRINT

REPRINTS
Telephone: 617-495-6192
Fax: 617-495-6985

Current and past articles are available, as is an annually updated index. Discounts apply to large-quantity purchases.

Please send orders to HBR Reprints, Harvard Business School Publishing Division, Boston, MA 02163.

HOW CAN *HARVARD BUSINESS REVIEW* ARTICLES WORK FOR YOU?

For years, we've printed a microscopically small notice on the editorial credits page of the *Harvard Business Review* alerting our readers to the availability of *HBR* articles.

Now we invite you to take a closer look at how you can put this hard-working business tool to work for you.

IN THE CORPORATE CLASSROOM

There's no more effective, or cost-effective, way to supplement your corporate training programs than in-depth, incisive *HBR* articles.

At just $3.50 a copy—even less for quantity orders—it's no wonder hundreds of companies use *HBR* articles for management training.

IN-BOX INNOVATION

Where do your company's movers and shakers get their big ideas? Many find inspiration in the pages of *HBR*. They then share the wealth by distributing *HBR* articles to colleagues.

IN MARKETING AND SALES SUPPORT

HBR articles are a substantive leave-behind to your sales calls. They add credibility to your direct mail campaigns. And demonstrate that your company is on the leading edge of business thinking.

CREATE CUSTOM ARTICLES

If you want even greater impact, personalize *HBR* articles with your company's name or logo. And put your name in front of your customers.

DISCOVER MORE REASONS IN THE *HBR CATALOG*.

In all, the *Harvard Business Review Catalog* lists articles on over 500 different subjects. Plus, you'll find collections, books, and videos on subjects you need to know. The catalog is yours for just $10.00. Order today. And start putting *HBR* articles to work for you.

How To Order. To order individual articles or the *HBR Catalog*, dial toll-free in the continental U.S. 1-800-545-7685. Outside the U.S. call 617-495-6192. **Please mention telephone code 165A** when placing your order. Or FAX your order to 617-495-6985. You may also send a check payable to Harvard Business School Publishing Division, or credit card information to: HBR Articles, Harvard Business School Publishing Division, Operations Department, Boston, MA 02163. **All orders must be prepaid.**

Order No.	Title	Qty. X	Price +	Shipping =	Total
21018	Catalog		$10		

U.S. and Canada: 5% for UPS or first class mail. *Foreign Surface Mail:* 15% for parcel post registered; allow 3–6 mos. *Express Deliveries (credit card orders only):* billed at cost; all foreign orders not designating express delivery will be sent by registered surface mail.

☐ Check enclosed (in U.S. funds drawn on U.S. bank)
☐ VISA   ☐ American Express   ☐ MasterCard

Card Number _____ Exp. Date _____
Signature _____
Telephone _____ FAX _____
Name _____
Organization _____
Street _____
City _____
State/Zip _____
Country _____

☐ Home address   ☐ Organization address
PLEASE REFERENCE TELEPHONE ORDER SOURCE CODE 165A

Harvard Business School Publishing

• SPECIAL COLLECTIONS • BOOKS • HBR ARTICLES • CUSTOM HBR ARTICLES • VIDEOS • CASES •